TRAUTEROSE

GROWING UP IN POSTWAR MUNICH

ELISABETH HAGGBLADE

GLASS**SPIDER**PUBLISHING

ISBN: 978-1-957917-34-4 (paperback)
ISBN: 978-1-957917-35-1 (e-book)

Library of Congress Control Number: 2023910375

Visit www.trauteroseauthor.com

Cover design by Judith S. Design & Creativity
www.judithsdesign.com
Published by Glass Spider Publishing
www.glassspiderpublishing.com

I am a part of all that I have met.
—"Ulysses," Alfred, Lord Tennyson

In this spirit, I wish to extend my thanks to all those to whom I owe my life:

My foster family and the foreign workers in their household in Salzgitter,

The nameless women in Munich who volunteered to take care of me,

The Catholic Sisters at the St. Anna Heim in Munich, to whom I owe my future.

Gott vergelt's [may God reward you for what you have done for me].

—Elisabeth Haggblade

Contents

Foreword

Everyone has a story to tell. Are we not all storytellers? What is our intent? Is mine to exorcise demons? Or settle a score? My intent is to focus on impressions I received from others based on their understanding of postwar conditions in Germany. The repeated comments about prosperous times I heard from people of all walks of life compelled me to describe my own experiences of growing up in Munich, because their thoughts and beliefs differ so greatly from mine. I was not alone in my judgment. I found my memory confirmed in my reading and research.

Much of what I felt during my early life in Munich has endured in my mind like a series of film slides, each image set in an unclear and foggy frame. For a time, I couldn't bring these pictures into focus, but they have stayed with me. The vagueness of my episodic memories cleared only with maturity.

The war stories of Vati, my foster father, serve as an example. I was too young to have been exposed to his narratives at the time. They were too brutal, but I came to be his only steady and faithful listener. He was lonely, as I was. Sharing his past with me became part of my story.

Giving a voice to other denizens near me in those early days meant drawing their portraits as I recall them. If their heirs living today find discrepancies in my sketches, they may be due to different interpretations by the respective storyteller. But all of them left footprints of the past that mingled with mine.

At war's end, the Allied military police conducted house-to-house searches looking for evidence betraying any German's past affiliation with the Nazi regime—be it a telling photo, an outdated party ID card, or a piece of an old uniform. Today, one can find such memorabilia at flea markets, but nothing is left of our *Gartenhäuschen* [garden hut] in Tivoli, nor of its contents.

I have no photos to share. The few I had I destroyed long ago in fits of depression. So I must draw with words to bring my anecdotal childhood memories into clearer focus.

The time I am describing consists of two parts. During my first eleven years, I lived with foster parents, a family diminished by the war and in the end destroyed by it through depression, illness, and death. Patrick Modiano, the French novelist and 2014 Nobel Prize winner born in 1945, is of my generation. His writing bears out that the war is never far from his mind.[1]

After my foster mother died, I could no longer stay with Vati because I was a minor. I spent the next seven years with Catholic Sisters at the *St. Anna Heim*, a home for children in

---

[1] Rachel Donadio, "Patrick Modiano, an Author of Paris Mysteries, Keeps His Own," *The New York Times*, November 1, 2015.

Munich, a time mostly shut off from the real world. In 1961, I emigrated from Germany, arriving in New York City on a windy day in March. I was eighteen years old.

All people and places described in this book are real. However, I have changed some names to protect the anonymity of potentially vulnerable individuals.

Introduction

How did my story begin? It's easier for me to narrate by reversing course and starting with my trip back to Germany in 2003 in an attempt to bring to a close an inconspicuous beginning.

My birth mother and Ludwig, her nephew by marriage, whom I'd just met for the first time, picked me up in his truck at the train station in Garmisch-Partenkirchen, because the express coach at that hour did not stop in the Bavarian Alpine village of Farchant, where they lived.

It was October. We quickly drove the three miles to my mother's house along autumn fields and trees with their brown dried leaves rustling on branches, past old-style Bavarian farmhouses and newer versions, balconies holding boxes with the last bright-red geraniums, and gardens showing golden dahlias and chrysanthemums tied with rope around propped-up sticks.

According to my fleeting observation of the few people milling about, Farchant's official census of about 3,500 inhabitants seemed greatly inflated. Where were they hiding? But Ludwig assured me that in addition to old-time Bavarian farm families, there were newcomers who commuted to

Garmisch or Munich for work.

What else did we talk about during that short drive? My mother remained silent, looking straight ahead. Ludwig, in his heavy Alpine brogue, offered pleasantries with a grin.

"*Ja, woast, uns geht's hoit guad* [We are doing well]."

It was my mother's eighty-fifth birthday. We had not been in contact with each other for about forty years. With life's clock running down, I wanted to reach her before her demise or mine. Sometime back, I had made fitful attempts at correspondence consisting of brief, vague messages of my whereabouts. After a year, I finally received a reply. Now I had invited myself to celebrate her special day.

More than that, though, I wanted to reckon with her. Why had she left me orphaned as a newborn for six months in a Munich hospital in the winter of 1942-43 and then handed me over to a foster mother with just a handshake?

At that stage of my life, I did not wish to be confrontational. I just wanted to know about her life. Were times really that bad during that winter? Why would my mother leave me when others kept their infants? (My war-widowed Russian professor, Helen Dmitriev, related to our class, years later, that she had taken her young daughter west across Siberia, on foot.)

When we arrived in Farchant, I could see that my long-gestating plan of seeking answers would be futile. Judging from the help for basic household tasks my mother requested of her nephew, and from her silence and unresponsiveness to her surroundings, I realized that she was suffering from Alzheimer's. There was no use even broaching my question.

The next day, wedged in her cushy living-room sofa corner, she surprised me by straightening herself suddenly and lighting into me with a clarion voice. "Forty years, you did not contact me, your own mother." From the abyss of her Alzheimer's fog emerged this outcry of reproach she had buried for decades.

My wound went deeper, I argued resentfully with myself. Should I counter her verbal outburst with the question, "Is it not a mother's first obligation to attend to her child before parent and child roles reverse with time?"?

Quickly, I checked my impulse. Did I have the right to probe my old, ill mother?

Instead, I tried to envision the time when she was twenty-four. According to records, it was the glacial winter of 1942-43 in Munich.

The Past: Inauspicious Beginnings

In the spring of 1943, the *städtische Krankenhaus* [municipal hospital] in Munich, urgently asked my mother to remove me from the orphanage section and find an alternative home for me. Anton, my Hungarian father, asked her to follow him to Budapest. She refused. My mother wanted to work to support herself. I was an extra burden.

Before my mother died, she related their last conversation to me, fitfully, in a few words. "No," she said to my father. "I will not follow you with the baby to Budapest. There is a war going on."

"As if there isn't one going on right here," he retorted.

"*Trotzdem* [Just the same]. I'm staying here," she said, not knowing that it would mean the end of their relationship.

My father, conscripted as an officer in the Hungarian army, left with his violin under his arm, or so I was told. He was the concertmaster in the entertainment orchestra of Barnabás von Géczy touring Europe. That is how they met. My father played in the same hotel where my mother worked.

After he left, my mother never heard from him again. He has been declared missing ever since, leaving behind a *Lehrstelle* [an emptiness] in my life. I have never seen a picture of him.

My father's entire history, as I know it, can be summarized in the single short paragraph I have just described.

Munich 1942-43

My mother was working as a waitress for the Café Luitpold. What other work would have been available to her as a graduate of the *Hotelfachschule* [hotel management school] at times like those? She was young and glamorous, her life in front of her, seemingly full of possibilities.

How, then, did I fit into her picture? I didn't. I was in the way. A brief encounter among women in a city tram one night came to the rescue.

When I was old enough, my foster mother vividly recalled the events for me. I visualized them thus unfolding.

My birth mother was riding the city tram, dozing as it rumbled through the dark winter streets. Inside the car, a dim yellowish light winked in tempo from a couple of bare light bulbs strung along the ceiling on a thin wire. A few scattered passengers wrapped in dark overcoats slumped on the hard wooden benches.

Two women sat in front of my mother, their hatted heads bent toward each other in subdued conversation. From them, she overheard shreds of phrases about the war's progress: "...*die Jungen bald heim von Russland* [the boys home soon from Russia]. *Der Hitler wird sie doch nicht in Russland lassen im Winter* [Hitler surely will not leave them in Russia in winter]," said the lady mummified in her Afghan lamb fur coat, seeking out her partner's eyes for hopeful confirmation.

"*Und Sie* [And you]?"

"*Keine Nachricht* [No news]," sighed the other lady, dressed only in a worn winter jacket, hat, and shawl. "*Der ältere in Warschau* [The older one in Warsaw]...*der jüngere in den Dolomiten* [the younger one in the Dolomites]—"

"*Darum möcht ich ein Mädel ham* [That's why I want a girl]," interrupted fur coat. "*Die wird bei mir bleim* [She'll stay with me]."

Those last words woke my mother in a flash out of her reverie. "*Ich hab eins—a Mädel* [I have one—a girl]," she blurted out, leaning forward between the two faces suddenly silent in astonishment.

My mother explained her plight. By the time the three women descended from the streetcar, fur coat had decided she wanted the young waitress's baby. A handshake and a planned trip to the hospital would seal my fate.

During the long months that my mother had left me at the birthing hospital, nourishment had been so poor that when my foster mother and her seventeen-year-old son saw me for the first time, covered with sores and crusts from secretions, he exclaimed, "Is she human or animal?"

Fur coat, my new foster mother, was a gentle Bavarian lady married to a master gardener, a former SS man in Hitler's army. They did not let the chaotic times prevent them from becoming my unofficial foster parents. They were near their fifties when they accepted me in 1943. They named me Traute, short for *Trauterose* [courageous rose], after the chanteuse Traute Rose, who had sung on the radio during the first world war. My new name was as unofficial as the adoption.

Salzgitter

In 1943, with me in tow, my foster mother, *Mutti* [muti] (short for "Mother"), followed my foster father, *Vati* [fati] (short for "Father"), from Munich to Salzgitter in Saxony in East Germany. Vati was Prussian by birth and upbringing. He had joined the *Schutzstaffel* [SS] early in the war. Both parents were ardent National Socialist (Nazi) supporters afflicted by the Hitler fever. They had even relinquished their wedding bands for the cause. "*Gold gab ich für Eisen* [I gave gold for iron]," was a nineteenth-century saying dating back to the Franco-Prussian War, gaining currency again during first and second world wars. Donated personal jewelry was melted down or sold, the proceeds used for weapon manufacturing.

Together, my foster parents operated a small farm in Salzgitter given to them by the Nazi Party, land probably appropriated earlier from Poland. To help with the chores of taking care of the household and the acreage with a little pond, the menagerie of chickens, ducks, and geese, they employed conscripted laborers sent to them by the party. A middle-aged Italian man worked in the yard, while two young Ukrainian women took care of the house and me. My first impressions were of the smiling faces of these ladies cradling me. I remember a tall sunflower standing next to my crib.

I began moving about as a toddler. When I stumbled into the pond, the Italian gardener fished me out when he saw part of my little dress protruding above the water. I was told later that he administered his version of first aid, causing me to vomit murky pond water and duck feces.

I owe my fleeting bliss in Salzgitter to Ukrainian caregivers, and I owe gratitude for a life saved to an Italian gentleman. I shall never know their names. I shall never see them again.

I shall never forget their kindness.

The Trek West

The war situation soon changed dramatically in eastern Germany with the German army, or what was left of it, retreating from the advancing Russians after the Battle of Stalingrad in 1943 and the siege of Leningrad in 1944.

My foster parents stayed in Salzgitter as long as they could. But they, too, had to leave, as so many Germans did, taking with them what they could carry, leaving behind everything else. They joined the refugee treks of thousands fleeing from east to west, a *Völkerwanderung* [mass migration] that swept everyone along in its wake: Germans leaving eastern provinces from territories being threatened by the advancing Russian army, Poles who did not wish to stay, prisoners of war of every stripe and nationality, released Jews, escaped

Jews, and slave laborers.

Any form of transportation would do: Wheelbarrows, carts of every type and size, hay wagons. Or one walked, as my foster parents did. Some had horses pulling tall carts laden with heavy furniture: Heirlooms of ornately carved commodes, wardrobes, a small cage for chickens squeezed in. An old lady who could no longer walk sat perched atop a chair or among cushions wedged in amid that load. Some who walked were leading by the hand an ailing relative or a child, perhaps with a goat trotting alongside, so I was told.

At that time, there were only a few roads leading away from the estates, farms, and villages. Pathways were jammed full of people with gear, moving along as quickly as their stamina and the human traffic would allow. Late arrivals had trouble merging into the seemingly endless throng of humanity forging ahead. As my foster parents described it, every hour was rush hour.

It was such a trek that Vati later memorialized in his wood carvings, explaining their history to me. He used birch wood panels he had cut from a neighbor's tree and prepared. He then edged in the scene with a pen knife. His creations showed the first rays of sun alighten on a semblance of figures emerging from a road between fields, the crush of humanity growing into three-dimensional silhouettes moving toward the viewer.

My foster parents described how they could hear the periodic thunder of Russian weapons exploding with flashes of lightning breaking up the dark sky on the horizon behind them. The migration continued off and on through the seasons. Hans von Lehndorff served as a doctor in Prussian villages and towns. He witnessed the siege and complete destruction of Königsberg (Kaliningrad) in 1945.

Von Lehndorff documented what he saw. During autumn, farms and fields were left unattended, including gardens with trees laden with ripe fruit and mature vegetable plots. Loose farm animals were breaking through yards stampeding harvest-ready fields, and cows were bellowing because no one was there to milk them.[2]

As the treks continued, there was snow now "reaching up to the bellies of horses pulling riders and carts westward," according to Marion von Dönhoff.[3]

On the side of the roads, the fleeing refugees averted their eyes from the dead sprawled out along the roadside: Clothed, unclothed, old, young, men, boys, women and girls who had been mistreated. According to rumor, which became only too true, no female between ages eight and eighty was safe from Russian rape attacks and massacres. The passersby bore witness as they passed through destroyed villages and towns: "...women nailed spread-eagled on barn doors,"[4] and "...pregnant women tied to trees and poles, disemboweled and left to die..."[5] This was Russian revenge—the wages of war.

---

[2] Hans von Lehndorff, "Ostpreussisches Tagebuch," (München: Hans Biederstein 1961), 8.
[3] Marion von Dönhoff, "Namen die keiner mehr nennt." (Köln: Eugen Diederichs, 1962), 34.
[4] Ibid, 19.
[5] Edgar Günther Lass, "Die Flucht: Ostpreussen 1944/45." (Bad Nauheim: Podzun, 1964), 277.

Suffering Less Often Described

The never-ending stream of displaced persons coming from the East added to the physical and psychological war damage in the West. What was the response that those thousands of refugees received in the western part of Germany? It should come as no surprise that they received less than a welcome from people who were survivors themselves trying to exist among ruins.[6]

And what did German soldiers who survived the fighting on the Front find upon returning home amid the rubble? Many did not want their wives back, because they had been violated by the Russians, damaged beyond proper healing. In turn, many German wives refused to take their husbands back. Not knowing whether the men were still alive, they had found other companions in the meantime. Some women did not even recognize their gravely ill, invalid menfolk and could not envision a postwar life with them. Those were constant themes of conversation overheard by my foster parents in the trams, in the food lines, across neighborhood fences, and discussed in our family.

Little was known about the high rate of suicides occurring during that time: Of men who could not face Germany's utter defeat, that all had been for nothing, that left only mayhem in its wake; of women who could not cope with the staggering loss of family, home, and community.

What was known about the couples who were still

---

[6] Arnold Taylor, "The forgotten story of when the Germans were the refugees," The Washington Post, September 3, 2015.

together? Even day-to-day duties had become overwhelming. Adi, my foster brother, told me that he had tried to help his friend, Horst, a POW returning from Russia.

Horst could not stand to listen to his wife washing dishes: "It sounds like machine gun fire to me," he said, leaving their apartment for good.

And the children? Many without parents were left to their own devices. Hiding in shelters, they had lived through the bombings. They had seen decimated neighborhoods, civilians killed. They had seen mutilated war veterans and haggard refugees searching for food and cover.

Severely disabled veterans were a common sight after the war. I saw men with amputated limbs transporting themselves on makeshift little carts that consisted of a few short boards with roller-skate-type wheels, pushing themselves along sidewalks with their stumps wrapped in rags tied with string.

While still of preschool age and riding in the tram one day, I vividly recall standing next to a man without a nose. He was holding a little girl with one hand and holding on to a ceiling strap with the other. Instead of a nose, two large dark holes opened in the middle of his scarred face. I was so shocked that I couldn't help staring at him for a minute. To this day, I can still feel his searing look aiming like a laser beam into my eyes. Such memories haunt children into adulthood and old age. Children see. Children hear. Children remember.

Even less has been written about the upheavals experienced by Germans who were displaced by the Russians from former Prussia. The pain suffered and the death toll of the eastern German people are still not widely discussed.

Their flight and subsequent expulsion that turned into genocide have never received wide public attention. "Millions cried, no one listened."[7]

The Russians took brutal revenge against their former foes, now their victims.

Beyond the bodily harm was the destruction of property. The *Junkers* [landowners] had lived in Prussia for generations. Many of them had been Hitler supporters and collaborators, but not all of them. Regardless, whoever was sucked into the spiral of war lost life and property. Their homes were demolished down to the last brick and hauled off to the East.

"Daily ten to fifteen trains loaded with everything and anything that could be dismantled (from German estates, homes, and farms) rolled east, returning empty."[8] The contents of their accumulated wealth—every piece of carved mahogany furniture, every exemplar of Meissner or Rosenthal porcelain, every item of Sterling silver, every lead crystal bohemian wine glass—all was transported to Russia; that is, if the spoils had not been demolished first by raging drunken Russian soldiers. How many of those pieces could still be found in Russian homes today, I wonder.

These refugees from the East were now landless, their recent life reduced overnight to a mere memory. Their stories became part of the timeless theme of forced flight, of total loss.

---

[7] PBS Broadcast email [from a woman], December 2018.
[8] Hans von Lehndorff, 206.

In and Out of Hitler's SS

So how did the Prussian SS officer, his Bavarian wife, and toddler Traute end up among the refugees? Because Vati was no longer a party member. Could a member just withdraw? No, he would be executed if he were to try. Vati's dismissal from the party was a story he told me when I was about thirteen years old. The tale left me startled then; it left me revulsed years later.

For some time during the war, Vati had been contemplating removing himself from the party when an episode provoked him. It was a repulsive incident that involved a British spy, a woman. She was caught and shot dead by SS men. As she lay on the ground, he witnessed these men abusing her body.

Vati wanted out of the party. One night, he was appointed door guard at a high-ranking SS function. Protocol was strictly prescribed. He was not to let anyone enter the building who was not in uniform or did not carry the requisite identification on him.

It was dark. A man in civilian clothes appeared at the door. Vati questioned him. The man told him in an arrogant manner that he did not have to answer him. After a short verbal exchange, neither party compromising, Vati seized him unceremoniously by the crotch and shoulder and heaved him onto the sidewalk.

The man filed a complaint with the highest order. It put the party in an uncomfortable position: Vati had obeyed the orders, but the man carried rank. The party determined that Vati should lose his rank and exit the SS. That action reduced him to one of many refugees in the long line heading west.

In and Out of Dachau

How had Vati survived the war years prior to and after his party dismissal? There were a couple of stories he shared with me later.

The first, told only *sotto voce*, involved cheating at a military medical exam during his early fighting days. He had a foreboding that the next battle would mean death. He was absolutely sure that time. Shooting himself in the foot would not do, so he took a chance in concocting a medical issue. From an abscess on his arm, he extracted a bit of pus and injected it into an open cut on his other arm. An attendant drew a blood sample that he determined to be contaminated enough to issue Vati a temporary exemption from combat. His premonition proved correct. The battle in question left no survivors.

Vati's second story about his dismissal from the SS took more convincing when the Allies searched everywhere for former Nazi collaborators after the war.

The Allies caught up with him in 1946. He was promptly hauled off to Dachau for detention. That was the very place where Jews had been incarcerated earlier. It was also the place where Vati had served as *Oberlagerführer* [chief] before the war began.

How long was he there? What were his duties in the Dachau camp during those early years? He let mail and packages addressed to the Jewish inmates pass through unchecked and unopened, he said. He did not elaborate. It never occurred to me to question him then. I would today. After the war, when he was interrogated by the American Military Tribunal, former Jewish inmates came to his defense, testifying favorably on his behalf during his trial.

While Vati was a political prisoner in Dachau in 1946, I well recall visiting him there with Mutti. We saw a sea of German prisoners in striped garb standing, sitting, or squatting on a large area of hard dirt with clumps of grass enclosed by barbed wire. He told us that American soldiers patrolling outside the fence encouraged the German men to stretch their hands through the wire to pluck dandelions to eat. When they did, the soldiers would shoot at them.

Vati was released from Dachau in 1947.

How does a former SS man adjust to life after that war? He could find only odd jobs: Trash hauler, night watchman, vacuum cleaner salesman.

The American Occupation

The American occupation forces stayed in Munich until 1955. I still recall their convoys driving along the street past our hut in Tivoli after the war. As soon as I heard the familiar low rumble of the diesel trucks, I ran out to watch them pass. I was elated by the soldiers' friendly waving and hollering. They even tossed out Hershey chocolate bars and other candy unfamiliar to me, all of which I gathered and devoured. Where did these nice men come from?

The newspapers showed quite a different face of American soldiers. Almost weekly, they reported a case of a GI raping a German woman.

Many years later, my Russian professor, Helen Dmitriev, described to me one harrowing scene she couldn't help overhearing. In the early 1940s, she had been sent to Bavaria to work for a farm family as a conscripted laborer. She had been an *Ostarbeiter* [a worker from the east], one of many Ukrainians who had been forced to leave their homes to work in Germany in 1941.

On her arrival in Bavaria, she was struck immediately by the neatness and orderliness of her new surroundings: Firewood stacked—as if by measure—outside the walls of the farmhouses, sun-bleached white linens folded and layered ever so evenly in the cedar chests, satiny many-pleated Trachten dresses (Bavarian Alpine costumes) lined up in closets. Helen's duties consisted of helping a mother and her two grown daughters run their household.

One day, Helen saw paratroopers drop from the sky and land near the property. Who were these men? They were soldiers in overalls, their many pockets filled with cigarettes and army paraphernalia, she recalled.

They entered the house. Helen fled to the attic, from which she heard the shouts and soul-rending screams of the three women being raped downstairs. The soldiers climbed up into the attic. Upon hearing that Helen could speak only a few Russian-tinged German words, they realized that she was not German and left her alone. It became quiet. Helen saw them leave. They did not take any of the Germans' belongings, as the Russians had done in the eastern part of Germany. They were American fliers, Helen learned.

Connected with the American occupation forces were

American women, perhaps relatives of soldiers. I caught my first glimpse of them later when I lived with the Catholic Sisters in Munich in the St. Anna Heim, a home for children. We noticed these ladies entering and exiting the PX (post exchange) located in the building directly across the street from ours, the former headquarters of the German Luftwaffe. We marveled at, and gossiped about, the fact that they showed up in public with hair curlers still in place. Their "painted" faces with makeup were considered almost indecent—more appropriate to nightclub performers, we thought—and they carried their purchases in common brown paper sacks instead of in sturdy European shopping bags with handles or in expandable nets. Their world was completely foreign to us.

Wirtschaftswunder [Economic Reconstruction]

The common assumption is that with the Marshall Plan and the proverbial German work ethic, a new and better life began immediately. That was true only for some.

The Marshall Plan was not implemented in Germany until 1949. In fact, famine was wide-spread between 1945 and 1949. Those were the *Hungerjahre* [hunger years]. Extra-low temperatures and a lack of *Lebensmittel* [food] led to the Hunger Winter of 1947-48. Food rationing continued in Munich until 1950. The deprivations in those years were greater for many than they had been during the actual war, because at that point there was truly nothing left. From my Kindergarten days, standing in line in front of the administration building, I still remember the soup ladled out from a barrel into our tin cups. A few grains of gray barley floated in it. The liquid tasted acrid and looked like something regurgitated.

Not all Germans went hungry, though. In plain sight, a certain segment of the population survived quite well, commensurate with its social circumstances. Those people were still living in their houses and villas, which, although hit by gunfire, still had enough walls and roof left to enable a semblance of normal, even dignified, existence.

Who were they? They were those who had held important positions in business, industry, and government prior to and during the war. They were playing important roles again, because in order to reconstruct Germany, the Allied occupation forces had to rely on Germans who knew where things were and how they functioned. It also helped if they knew some English, learned perhaps as POWs in the United States toward the end of the war or afterward. The United States government wanted to build a democratic Germany as a bulwark against Communist Russia.

There were also private individuals who managed well. In this category, I include people I saw depicted in a newspaper photo years later. An older gentleman and a young woman, both dressed in well-cut winter coats, were pushing an upright piano on a small wooden platform on wheels along a street lined on both sides with the rubble of bombed out buildings. Evidently, there were still people who could afford to worry about saving a piano.

One neighborhood example of economic reconstruction was the local shoemaker. In a dark niche of his shop, he used to sit on his wooden stool with a shoe-paste-smeared apron tied on, never looking up to greet the entering customer, always bending his grimly determined face and black-stained fingers over a boot or shoe that was hardly worth fixing.

A year or so later I met him again, but this time in his new shoe store, a bright, glassy affair with polished woodwork on the walls and entry door, shelves displaying new shoes of every size and color. Dressed in new finery, he was standing proudly behind the cash register. His beaming face portrayed his newfound success and obvious happiness. He was effusively greeting customers. He had become a different man. How did this transformation happen? Had he perhaps benefited from reimbursements that the Allies allocated to certain people for war-damaged goods?

One of the first noticeable signs of better times ahead was the seemingly overnight disappearance of mutilated veterans, as if they had been swept away to make room for the new Germany in which there was no place for such pitiful sights. My assumption was that many had died from their severe injuries by then, while others had begun to have access to improved medical care.

Some certainly did recover; others did not. Who were the people who did not profit from the *Wirtschaftswunder?*

Those who were too old and too sick to make the transition. That was us and many others.

Those who had lost all and who struggled to keep alive, hoping for the occasional menial job, collecting refuse and cleaning it. Those with only a makeshift roof over their heads. Those without connections, without the support of better-off relatives. That was us and many others.

Those who were incapable of switching political sides like chameleons, as some did. Those who could not adjust to the new reality of a lost war. Those who had believed in the Hitler system and had gone down with the ship. Those who accepted the defeat as their lot. That was us and many others.

Those who were damaged physically and psychologically beyond rehabilitation. That was us and many others.

PART I: TIVOLI
(1945-1954)

Chapter I: A Small Neighborhood at the Edge of Munich

My foster parents' flight from Salzgitter ended in Munich during the last bombing raids in the winter of 1944-45.

To make ends meet, they rented a small apartment and a hole-in-the-wall shop in an old building at the eastern edge of Munich. They sold milk, bread, *Semmeln* [rolls], and, when available, butter and cheese. To purchase milk from them, one brought one's own container, such as a large bottle or a jug. The milk was ladled out with a zinc measuring cup shaped like a cylinder on a long handle. Dairy products were unpasteurized. It was possible to leave milk in a container for several days, and it would turn into decent yogurt.

Mutti was supposed to keep track of the inventory, but when it fell short, Vati ranted and raved, assuming that she had been reading one of her beloved romance novels—of unknown provenance—on the sly instead of paying attention to her duties.

But the war put a sudden stop to their shop that left Vati no choice but to return to gardening, his former profession, using a weekender garden plot with a hut he had rented for about ten dollars a month in today's currency. The land belonged to Tivoli, on the outskirts of town. That piece of dirt was to become a major source of food for us during the postwar years.

It was Mutti who had a premonition that they would not survive in their apartment unless they were to relocate permanently to the garden plot, and she meant immediately. A day later, the entire city block containing their old apartment and shop was leveled by Allied bombs.

Adi, my foster parents' youngest son, joined us there in 1947 after his release in Ireland as POW.

Tivoli

Coming home from school, turning on Hirschauer Strasse, I passed a park, the *Englische Garten* [English Garden], on the left, and on the right a women's clinic fenced in by a concrete wall with wrought iron posts, and behind them a small park of chestnut trees shading a neglected lawn.. Around the corner from the clinic still stood a couple of stone villas undamaged by the war. Across from them, a wide meadow opened the view toward the weekender gardens and huts, with the tall dark gray towers and industrial buildings of the Tivoli mill looming behind them. I could spy our garden hut from there. I was home.

Tivoli was the name of a working mill situated next to a swiftly running stream, the Eisbach. Its waters were, and still are, dangerous because of the cold temperatures, fast currents, and tricky swirls. Today, this stream is a favorite with surfers. It still occasionally claims a life.

The mill owned the square-mile meadow and about half a dozen 900-square-foot weekender garden plots, called *Schrebergärten*[9] [weekender gardens], some with 450-square-foot huts, rented out for a pittance. During the postwar years, most parcels belonged to absentees, except for a few hardscrabble occupants for whom that piece of dirt was a life saver. It allowed for the planting of vegetables and fruit trees, thus providing sustenance during those difficult times. Officially, no one was supposed to live in the huts. They were meant for storing garden tools and for sitting in the shade, or for waiting out a rain. But in the 1940s and 1950s, poor people actually lived there, with the mill turning a blind eye. Today, the *Schrebergärten* are highly in demand as hobby gardens with city dwellers.

Living in Tivoli meant existing in a bare-bones hut that contrasted with the surrounding bounteous beauty of nature in our garden, in the deserted overgrown neighborhood gardens, in a meadow undisturbed by human traffic outside

---

[9] Named after Moritz Schreber (1808-1861), who created allotment gardens as a place of recreation for children.

our garden gate, in the English Garden across the street, with its winding paths among an endless variety of grasses and weeds, wild flowers, fungi, bushes, and trees offering towering canopies, blossoms and seeds, or frost-bejeweled branches swaying in the winter breeze, snow-padded tree branches exposing their black barrenness beneath—all according to season.

The Place: The Outside - Our Garden Plot

Our place began at the edge of a sharp bend in the street. A short path led to the picket fence and gate that Vati had built with discarded lumber. Outside the fence grew a pretty spruce that he covered in winter with refuse from our outhouse—feces and bits of paper—meant to discourage a thief quick with a handsaw, who may have wanted a *Tannenbaum* [Christmas tree]. During cold winter months, these dung decorations froze solid on the branches, disguised by the frost and snow. Come spring, however, the tree steamed during the thaw when the sun melted all.

The Yard

Whenever he could, Vati brought home roots, bulbs, and seedlings from abandoned properties that resulted in exuberant plantings of phlox, delphinium, iris, an apple tree, and a sour cherry that would greet the visitor entering through the gate. To the right of the path leading toward the hut were vegetable beds of carrots, cabbage, rhubarb, kohlrabi, onions, a few potato plants, and parsley, and a plum and a pear tree. On the other side, next to the hut, grew white and red currant, blackberry, and gooseberry bushes left standing by previous occupants, which he trimmed to manageable size. During spring thaw and in the summer heat, a large compost heap smoked in the far corner of the yard.

The Arbor

In one corner of the yard, on slightly higher ground, Vati and his son, Adi, built a round wooden table and a half-circle bench, placing them in such a way that the view opened to the garden and beyond. For cover, he bent and tied the branches of elderberries growing there so that they formed a thick canopy.

On both sides near the arbor thrived jasmine bushes, thin, gray, straight sticks in winter, fragrant bows of white blossoms with yellow stamens that attracted bees in late spring and summer. We often sat there listening to their drone as they weaved in and out of swaying branches, their "thighs" thick with pollen. On hot days, the satin petals of peonies and their swollen buds were drooping, the scent of blossoms intoxicating as if nature had exhaled deeply, giving off its perfume. No leaf was stirring, nature holding still as if any move were an exertion. Even the birds checked their song. They sat in the grass with their beaks open as though gasping for air. Only the bees worked tirelessly, and the ants—if disturbed.

On special occasions, we sat under the arbor with a cup of coffee and *Bienenstich* [bee sting], a dessert. The pastry consisted of two layers of light, spongy dough separated by a layer of vanilla pudding, topped with stiff cream and burned almond sugar. It was a big treat that was also sought by the bees, hence the name *Bienenstich*. Attracted to the sugar, bees, wasps, and bumble bees swarmed around our plates, noshing on the sugar coating. We had to be careful not to swallow an insect along with a bite of cake.

Always intrigued by flowers, I wandered around and sought out the deep blue iris with its yellow "beard." I wanted to touch, stick my finger into its center, but when Vati caught me, he said, "*Nein, das ist verboten* [Don't touch]!"

The Terrace

With rock debris collected from Allied bombing rubble in town, Vati and Adi raised the area in front of the hut into a makeshift terrace. Above it stood the clothesline where in winter our laundry hung frozen stiff as boards, men's shirts looking like upside-down scarecrows. I learned the hard way about the fragility of fabric in that condition. It would tear so easily when I was not careful in removing it from the clothes pins.

Below the terrace was a hand pump, our only source of water. In winter, we first had to prime it by adding some warm water to break the ice that had accumulated inside. Once partially melted, we could raise and lower the long steel handle a few times to get it going. We carried the pumped water in a five-gallon bucket up the wooden steps into the kitchen, often my assignment.

The Outhouse

Our eliminations took place in a tiny outhouse without a door. Vati and Adi built it in the farthest corner in the backyard. To block it from an outsider's view, they covered the corner fence parts with corrugated sheet metal. Inside the outhouse, neat squares of old newspapers we had trimmed from discards gathered at public trash heaps hung suspended from a string attached to a nail in the wall. Sitting on the wooden toilet seat, I was terrified of slipping into the big drum below, with caterpillars and vermin crawling over our droppings and up the wall toward the opening where I sat. Outside in winter, yellow-stained paths in the snow from the men's standup routine of "wild pissing" lined the right angles by the fence.

And what did we do with the outhouse refuse? The men periodically emptied the big container and fertilized our vegetable beds with the spread. In summer, I often squatted amid the plants, chewing a raw kohlrabi like a rabbit. I always wanted to eat.

The Hut: Our Garden House - The Structure

My foster parents' plot included a hut that had been constructed amateurishly, perhaps in haste, by a previous occupant or occupants. Who were they? Where did they come from? Why did they leave? What was their story? In the makeshift "garrett," I once saw a long, white tulle dress among the dust and cobwebs. Was it a dance robe or a bridal gown? In touching it carefully, I felt connected to its previous owner. I fantasized about her. She must have been tall and slender. Was she beautiful? Silence keeps its secrets.

The hut consisted of disintegrating layers of brick covered with crumbling, rough white coating, and a wooden roof with some rotting boards. To repair the damage wrought by time and neglect, Vati and Adi collected bricks and wood pieces still intact from the *Trümmerhaufen* [war waste material] in town and carted them home in a rickety handcart, a distance of about a mile or two, depending on the location of the trove they found. They laid chicken wire fence pieces across the slanting sides of the roof and poured a home-made version of concrete across to stabilize it.

Attached to the end of the hut in the back was a "veranda," as we liked to call it. Wooden planks covered the floor, corrugated aluminum walls rose up to one's waist, and glass-house-type windows—some cracked, others missing—led to a flat roof covered with pieces of tar paper. A worm-eaten ladder with uneven steps leaned against the outside wall. Sitting on that roof on clement mornings with no one in sight, I could observe the dew-drenched flora all around, the rising sun climbing through treetops in the nearby English Garden. All were sights of wonder, Zen-like moments for me.

The Inside: Rooms Bearing Witness

There was no electricity in the hut for the first nine years of our stay. We used kerosene lamps and candles. We had no running water. The hand pump in the yard served as our fresh water source until the very end. Our two rooms, kitchen-cum-living room, and bedroom, measured about 450 square feet.

The Kitchen

From the entry, a painted wooden door opened to the kitchen. In winter, Vati suspended a dark grayish horsehair blanket hooked on nails above the door to keep the cold air out.

Inside, on the right stood a wash bowl on a little wooden stool with a piece of *Kernseife* [cord soap], the men's combs and toothbrushes next to it.

Above the bowl, a ten-by-ten mirror looked down from the wall, and a towel hung from a nail on the left. The wall registered accumulated faded stains of ablutions, along with a few dried dark spots of flies' residue.

Daily grooming in our crowded wash corner in the kitchen was an effort. The men often ended up with minor cuts in their faces as they were trying to shave in pale light while looking into the cloudy mirror. They stuck pieces of transparent cigarette paper or newspaper on their open cuts to stem the trickles of blood. Once the blood dried, the tiny paper bits flaked off.

A coal- and wood-burning stove occupied the opposite corner of the kitchen. A dented aluminum teapot, always containing some water, rested permanently on the steel cooktop that showed a crack angling toward the stove pipe. A small window above the stove faced a neighbor's yard. A huge poplar, whose trunk we could touch through that open window, caused concern whenever a summer lightning storm hit. We counted the seconds between thunder bursts to judge lightning proximity. Opposite the stove stood a tall cupboard, Coke bottle glass doors hiding an assortment of dishes that included a cup or two with missing handles, a sugar bowl without a lid, a porcelain coffee can with a partially broken-off spout.

The Bedroom

Another blanket served as a curtain separating the kitchen from the bedroom that contained two beds on steel frames and a small bed for me pushed against one corner of the wall. During heavy rains, the roof tended to leak above my parents' bed. Once, they placed a bucket in the middle of their bed to catch the leak. While taking a nap on it one time, I nudged the bucket in my slumber, tipping cold water over me and the bed. We wiped it all up, and my parents slept there again as usual.

In a corner of the bedroom stood a small commode with a bowl and a water jug. Mutti and I stored our toilet utensils next to them. In winter, the water left overnight in the half-gallon jug froze solid. We heated water on the kitchen stove to melt the ice enough so we could at least wash our faces. A washcloth dipped in the bowl and a bit of *Kernseife* served the purpose. Water splashed about as we flipped the wet washcloth around our necks.

The bedroom had a large window facing the yard. During the cold season, all windows froze shut and showed the most wondrous ice flowers and crystals on the windowpanes. They were tall sheath-like creations with thick, phantasmagorical blooms.

The Kitchen Table: Table Talk

The kitchen table was our universe. Most of what we said and did took place on it or around it. It heard more than just our daily clattering with dishes and assorted table settings.

The table bore witness to an angry Vati, who made every

plate and fork dance and jump while he pounded the tabletop with his fist, bellowing because I was late for a meal. Playing at the neighbors about half a block away, I had not heard his distinctive whistle. The third whistle was the limit—it meant trouble. He never struck me, then, but he came so close that I could hardly control my bladder. All the while, a small, frameless copy of Jean-François Millet's *The Angelus* looked down on us from the wall next to a framed headshot of Vati's parents at their golden wedding anniversary. His parents, shoulder pressed to shoulder, looked sternly straight ahead— father in high collar, mother in a dress buttoned-up to the neck, and mutton sleeves.

Less violent, but fearsome nonetheless, were discussions and arguments around the table, mostly about money. There were notifications from the Tivoli mill about past-due rent, concerns about Mutti's serious health issues resulting from strokes, or orders from my elementary school teachers to buy school supplies.

Each new school year began with painful scenes around our table because Vati was beside himself when I came home with requests. The administration provided textbooks, but each pupil was to bring notebooks, pencils, a ruler, an eraser, crayons, India ink, a penholder, and pens. The teachers were exacting. Notebooks, for example, had to be color-coordinated. A set of six notebooks, one for each subject, required a paper cover with a matching plastic overlay. We had to go to a stationery store for those supplies. "And how are we going to pay for these?" Vati demanded to know, more to himself than to me.

The German tradition of strict school requirements continues to this day, although even more elaborate than in the past. For example, in 2019, a primary district in Berlin gave parents "a school-sanctioned two-page shopping list of supplies that includes, among other items, three pencils of precisely increasing hardness, a ten- to twelve-centimeter plastic ruler. These supplies were to be carried in a prerequisite standard bag that costs about $275.00."[10]

But there were pleasant moments, too, around our kitchen table in Tivoli. By then, I was about eleven years old, old enough to participate in some diversion. The occasion could be a holiday, a birthday, or simply a change in mood, a need to create our own entertainment. After the evening meal, instead of getting up, Vati might remain seated, as if contemplating something.

We did not play cards; we didn't have any. Whatever books the family owned had been destroyed during the Allied bombing raids. *Tante Meta* [Aunt Meta], Vati's sister who came to us after Mutti died from a massive stroke when I was ten years old, recited from memory examples of Friedrich Schiller's classical poetry. Vati played German folk songs on his harmonica and sang in between with me, while Adi hummed along. And the adults told stories of their youth. That was when they actually laughed. The present made us rather sober.

---

[10] Christopher F. Schuetze, "In Germany, The Weight Of Learning Is Felt Early," The New York Times, September 9, 2019.

The Kitchen Table: Table Work

Every activity took place on the table because there was no other place to work: Preparing food, such as cleaning and cutting vegetables and meat—if there was any—and slicing bread and cheese. There was also eating, ironing, and writing.

Preparing

Tante Meta and I prepared our garden vegetables for cooking. She oversaw my work, making sure that I scraped and peeled off only the thinnest layer of skin from potatoes for the mashed version. We ate the meat with every scrap of fat and gristle left intact.

Eating

Cabbage stew and potato soup with carrots, kohlrabi, leeks, and onions were our mainstay. Meat was available only once a week, with most of it reserved for the men. We ate *Bauernbrot* [farmer's bread], dark-brown, rough round loaves that lay flat.

Butter, when we had it, was *Bauernbutter*, unpasteurized and watery. It tasted like only *Bauernbutter* can taste, namely of cow shed. Milk at that time was also unpasteurized. When it curdled, it became yogurt. For coffee, we drank *Ersatz*, made of grains. Tante Meta baked delicious *Kuchen* [cakes], such as *Himbeerkuchen* [raspberry cake] or *Torten* [tarts or pies], depending on the berries, rhubarb, and plums from our yard when in season.

I recall once eating my first orange—a gift from a visitor, who peeled it slowly, with reverence, at our table. What a wondrous fruit, I thought, to come wrapped in its own upholstered shell!

Food articles were placed in our "refrigerator," a cupboard in the kitchen corner. Next to *Eingemachtes* [home-canned food], such as pickled cabbage or gooseberry jam, lay raw vegetables from the garden, such as cucumbers, some rhubarb sticks, and a couple of potatoes. On hot days, the heat dried out the bread too quickly, while the cheese became over-ripe.

One day, Vati placed on the kitchen table a small saucer holding a round, thin, cardboard box without a lid, the kind containing wedges of about eight ounces of Camembert, a common, inexpensive cheese at that time, but a treat for us. A couple of pieces were missing. Another wedge lay open. He offered that one to me with a gesture of benevolence. I took one look at it and saw the inside of its white mold rind filled solid with yellowish, fat, thick maggots stirring sluggishly. I pointed, but Vati said that I was seeing things. Disbelieving, he picked up that piece and swallowed it in a couple of bites, chiding me for refusing his offer.

Ironing

After Tante Meta had joined us in Tivoli, she ironed on the kitchen table, never getting a spot on the clean laundry. With a towel laid beneath, she ironed the men's slacks by wringing out a cloth the size of a large handkerchief, spreading it across part of a pant-leg, then placing the hot iron in a steamy sizzle on top of the protecting cloth to press in a sharp crease. Tante Meta knew how to do it without ruining the initial crease.

Ironing men's white cotton shirts presented a different challenge. (Each man owned one such shirt.) She began with the collar, then the button strips, the cuffs, the sleeves—one at a time. She ironed each front panel, working up to the shoulder part, and lastly the back. How did she do it without crumpling the ironed sections in the process and without getting a smudge from the cast-iron appliance that was heated on the coal-and-wood stove? Before Tante Meta came to us, I remember seeing Vati bent over the kitchen table ironing his own slacks in the same way.

(I still iron like this today, but with an ironing board. When my hot iron meets the damp cloth laid over the garment, the faintly singed vapor reminds me of my early days in Tivoli.)

Writing

The kitchen table witnessed my laborious attempts at cleaning off crumbs and specks from the waxen tablecloth before attempting to write my school assignments. But no matter how hard I tried, it never failed that a big, fat spot ended up on my notebook, which the teacher encircled with her red pencil, the red matching my burning cheeks in embarrassment when she pointed to it in class.

And ever present was the flytrap dangling from the ceiling above the kitchen table. It consisted of a band two inches wide, a foot and a half long, covered with honey-like glue. One twisted it out of a tightly rolled paper casing and hung it up. The yellow spiral took no time to darken to brown and then to black from flies caught in the paste. The trap slowly oscillated in the breeze. Some flies, with their backs stuck in the glue, were still trying to move their spindly legs in the air until their corpses loosened from the sticky mass and dropped with a dry pin click onto the waxen tablecloth.

The Stove

We treated the stove in the corner with more respect than our kitchen table. One could get burned easily by touching it carelessly. Sometimes, the stovetop would glow red hot when fed too many wood or coal pieces during an extra-cold winter evening.

But it was our hearth. Vati would start the fire every morning with kindling and crumpled pages of old newspapers he had found in trash bins on his way home from his night watch job. The tinder, brush, and wood logs that he and Adi gathered, cut, and split, came from our yard. Or maybe we helped ourselves to stray pieces left in an absentee neighbor's yard. It was not uncommon for some neighbors to leave their garden plots unattended for months at a time.

The stove was like a warm beast that exuded heat to warm us and to cook our meals, but it was not as silently tolerant as our kitchen table was. It rebelled if not treated properly. It coughed up smoke when the wood logs that Vati shoved into its opening were still a bit green, or when the coals were damp. It gave off a warning hiss before shutting down. The accumulated soot often needed to be removed from the stovepipe that rose from the corner upward with a horizontal extension poking through the wall to the outside. When it had enough of our mistreatment, the kitchen quickly filled with dense fumes.

And the stove listened. It overheard plenty of our daily travails. It was not patient with me when I fed it wood pieces with one hand, while with the other I tried to stir a large pot filled with a bubbling mass of stewing berries for jam. We had just a few red currant and gooseberry bushes in the yard, but they produced prodigiously. It was my job to pick and clean the berries. The currants were easy to harvest. I slid my hand lightly down each branchlet to remove the clusters. Gooseberries were harder to deal with because they were hidden among thorny branches. With scissors, I snipped off the tiny, wilted, dried-up blossom leftovers and stems from each berry, and I rinsed them well. Snacking took place unobtrusively.

We poured the berry mass into a large pot placed on top of the stove. Tante Meta added water and sugar and heated it. The *Hexenbrühe* [witch's brew] needed to be stirred constantly with a wooden spoon until it was reduced to a viscous mass. But as soon as I slowed down or even let up stirring, fiery hot bubbles shot up like miniature volcanoes that had a way of landing on my hands and arms, leaving red blotches and burn marks. I cried out. I was ten years old and had a hard time mustering the patience to stand by the stove for long periods.

The Sofa

Against the wall behind the kitchen table stood a dark upholstered sofa, provenance unknown. That piece of furniture, too, was witness to our daily tribulations. I often sat next to Adi, my foster brother, sliding helplessly into the deep spot his body dug into that worn contraption.

He lingered near me with the usual pieces of cigarette paper stuck on his cheeks left from shaving marks. I teased him. A little pack of thin paper squares usually lay around for the men to roll cigarettes. They commonly picked up discarded cigarette stubs left by the street gutters or on sidewalk edges. At home, they opened these rejects, spilled the leaf bits onto a little plate, filled a square of that fragile cigarette paper with them, rolled it up tight, folded over the edge, and licked it shut. Sometimes a bit of tobacco would protrude and zing up in a tiny flame as they lit their "new" ciggy.

Tante Meta and I sat on the sofa for hours in the evening, mending clothes, letting out seams of garments to enlarge them, repairing stockings and socks by weaving over threadbare areas and holes.

The sofa was also my sick bed. I dimly recall lying there during one hot night by the foggy yellow light of a candle on the kitchen table. Vati shirtless, suspenders dangling from his pants, was bending his stooped, hirsute chest over me, placing one cold compress after another on my feverish forehead.

I had been quite ill and had missed at least a week of classes. Was it diphtheria or scarlet fever? The school became concerned and sent a classmate to check on me. Who thought she would be able to find us, located as we were away from any residential area? But she did find us, to my embarrassment. I was loath for my schoolmates to see how precariously we lived.

Chapter II: Portraits of Family Members and Neighbors

Who were the people who populated our corner of Tivoli? There were those who lived there: Mutti and Vati (my foster parents), Adi (their youngest son), and I, Traute. There were the relatives who came to visit occasionally, namely Siegfried (the middle son); and those who came for extended stays, like Tante Meta (Vatis' sister), and Herbert (the oldest son). There was also someone who never came, but who played a large role in our lives. That was *Tante Anette* [Aunt Anette], Mutti's sister. And there were our neighbors, both good and not so good.

Mutti

I have only abbreviated recollections of the person to whom I owe the most. Mutti was long suffering before she died in 1952 at age fifty-seven from a final stroke.

My first memory of her is when she was pushing me in a baby carriage across a bridge spanning the Schwabinger Bach, a brook in Munich. It must have been in 1946. The bridge was dilapidated. Through wide gaps between rickety boards,

I could see the water rushing below. Wire strung helter-skelter held more such boards together in a makeshift railing. All of that criss crossed wire around the floor and sides was meant to prevent anyone from crossing it, but Mutti managed nonetheless.

My second memory recalls her begging for bread. Farmers in the outlying regions of Munich had at least a way of feeding themselves during that time, and Mutti knew that. Together, we took the train to the nearest village and walked from farm to farm. She took me by the hand as we followed country roads hemmed in by fields and meadows. It was summer. It was hot. We wiped sweat off our faces.

The farmhouses were typical Bavarian buildings with white stucco walls, some dirtied at the bottom from rain splatters or mud from dogs, pigs, cows, a horse or two. Carved dark wooden balconies showing a few geraniums, a huge overhanging pitched wooden roof covering it all. The whole place reeked of the earthy smell of farm animals, the dung heap, mildewed straw, and the slightly acidic smell of sloshing milk spilled from containers standing about or from milked cows. It was a smell that penetrated everything: The houses outside and in, farmers' skin, their hair, their clothes, and, if truth be known, their underwear—as I found out during subsequent visits. All of that started to change a few years later with farm practices conforming to modern methods.

During the postwar years, farmers were suspicious and unwelcoming to strangers. As Mutti and I approached a house, the farmer's wife typically stuck her head out of a little window near the front door, asking, "*Wos wuist denn* [What do you want] (Bavarian with the informal "you" condescending toward Mutti)?

"*A Stückl Brod füa mei Kloa* [A piece of bread for my little one]," Mutti said.

The farmer's wife closed the window and took a while before she opened the door, motioning to Mutti to open her shopping net (a loose-knit type of expandable bag). The woman dropped in a couple of rough pieces of dark bread, which she most likely had baked for her family. With a hearty "*Dankschön*," Mutti and I left to continue our quest. Some of the farmers' wives were generous so that after a few more stops, Mutti was able to carry away two shopping nets bulging with bread heels. I was about five years old, too little to be of much help. Exhausted, we walked the long way back to the train station, rode sleepily on the wooden bench in the compartment, and then walked from the station to our hut. It was a long day. But we had bread.

Mutti also knew how to save something from my graspy hands. Bartlett pears were ripening in our garden. She selected the most mature and left them in a bowl on the kitchen table. I was old enough by then to help myself to them. but they had not yet achieved their luscious ripeness. Mutti caught me and simply placed them out of my reach, lining them up on the uppermost shelf in the kitchen. Later, she chose one when it was at its peak and handed it to me. I have never forgotten the taste of that yellow pear, its thin skin breaking in my bite, juice flowing down my fingers and covering my hands.

I don't know why Mutti gave me her red garnet ring one day, the only piece of jewelry she had left. The red center stone was surrounded by tiny white crystals, all of it encased in silver. Perhaps she felt her end nearing and wanted me to have it. I wore it to our third-grade class. I liked twisting it around one of my fingers, playing with it during class. It came off, fell to the floor, and rolled away. I was too timid to ask the teacher for permission to look for the ring beneath my desk. It would have meant interrupting class, so I waited till the school bell rang at the end of the hour. But by that time, I had forgotten about the ring. When I finally thought of it the next day and looked for it between classes, I could not find it. It was gone. I was too young to appreciate Mutti's gift.

I lost other things, too; mittens, for example. To prevent misplacing them, children's mittens were attached to a string slipped underneath a winter coat's collar and through the armholes. Out of each cuff dangled a safely attached mitten. How could we lose them? String with mittens and scarves, all had a way of dropping to the floor as we hurriedly pulled off our coats in the wardrobe before going to class. Their loss was usually not noticed until we left the warm classroom, just as hurriedly, and headed home.

I kept on losing mittens. Mutti would despair with my negligence. We had barely enough to eat, yet I was so careless. On several occasions, she walked the mile or so to an apartment house nearer to town where a store was located on the ground floor. The owners lived above it, as it was customary then. Usually after store hours, Mutti walked up the flight of stairs, knocked on their door, and begged them to sell her another pair of mitts, or perhaps they let her have them on credit. I can't ever recall being reprimanded for my repeated thoughtlessness.

From these past experiences, though, I have retained an unnatural fear of losing things that still grips me today. I am beside myself when something is missing, only to find that I had merely misplaced it or that it was in its rightful place all along.

A drive by an elementary school in the California foothills at the end of a school year in the 1970s put a different spin on my guilt-ridden past. Surrounding the school was a picket fence with assorted winter items greeting the passerby from each stake: A glove here, two mittens there (each perched on a separate picket), a shawl twisted around one, a cap riding on top of another, even a coat draped over a peg, a merry array.

My companion explained that those colorful items were not necessarily "lost" but considered simply undesirable because of color, fit, or appearance. Those were different economic times, indeed, from those I knew from my childhood.

Mutti's health was seriously deteriorating in the early 1950s. In Tivoli, in good weather, she spent much time sitting under the arbor of elderberries in our yard, staring out into the open. By then severely disabled through a series of strokes, she had trouble walking. Instead of speaking, she could only come up with grunting sounds and point with her hand, and that with difficulty. On hot summer days, sweat ran down the sides of her face, dripping from the tips of the crudely cut dark gray hair onto her neck. She sat mostly with her hands folded in her lap, never complaining, sometimes sighing.

Mutti became incontinent, a grievous condition that weighed heavily on me, because I was supposed to take her to mass on Sundays at the Catholic Church in Bogenhausen, another part of town. I tried to get out of my obligation as often as I could, because I was embarrassed to take her. She tended to stop in the middle of the sidewalk, urine running down her legs. To what degree was she aware of her situation, if at all? But I was well aware of how the Catholic Church condemned a person for preventing a believer from attending services. It was guilt I carried around with me for years. Today, I feel greater guilt toward my foster mother for not having been more helpful to her than I do for not having adhered to the canon of the church.

One summer night on our veranda, Mutti suffered her final stroke. She fell like a tree. I fully expected to see a large dent in the wooden floorboards, because the impact was so heavy. Mutti lay motionless. All of us were numb.

I assume that Vati had to ride his bike to our physician, Dr. Raab, ringing his doorbell in the middle of the night. The doctor lived in an old apartment building with his office below on the ground floor.

Dr. Raab was a large, dignified gentleman in his late sixties, with receding pitch-black hair and dark hooded eyes. He always treated us with respect. He never rushed us during our infrequent office visits even though we were merely *Kassen Patienten* [privately uninsured patients] (the state paid for our medical treatment.) That night, Dr. Raab answered the doorbell himself, but he sent a young intern to us.

What was this young doctor thinking when he saw our hut,

where he had to bend low to get through the door into our kitchen and from there to the veranda where Mutti lay? What happened next? I don't recall. Vati and I visited Mutti in the hospital the next day. Communication was impossible. She stirred slightly upon hearing my name. That was all. Mutti died a few days later at age fifty-seven in 1952. I was ten years old.

Mutti's Funeral

The service and interment took place at the Nordfriedhof cemetery in Munich. Vati, in his grief, had cut every flower in our yard. He wound them into a wreath, which he carried over his shoulder as the three of us—Vati, Adi, and I—walked to the tram station. It was a long ride to the destination stop on the Ungererstrasse. We still had to walk past the flower shops and headstone workshops lining the sidewalk. The flowers in Vati's wreath started to wilt and loosen.

In the postwar years during the winter holidays of All Saints and All Souls on November first and second, respectively, these shops carried *ewiges Licht* [eternal light] for graves. The light consisted of a candle pressed into a holder surrounded by a red plastic sheath that would glow when the candle was lit. On those holidays, war widows draped in their black fur coats and hats resembled dark silhouettes moving in a long line on the sidewalk as they slowly made their way to the cemetery gate, each carrying candle lights and chrysanthemums to the graves of their relatives.

On the day of Mutti's funeral in August 1952, Vati, Adi, and I were the only ones on that sidewalk. We reached the

Nordfriedhof's Byzantine-style portico, which is still recognizable today from Thomas Mann's description in his novella *Death in Venice*, first published in 1912.

We entered the bronze gate of the funeral hall and turned left into the corridor. Behind a glass wall, the dead were lined up in their funeral attire in open caskets. Embalming was not customary in Germany then and still is not standard today. The upper part of each casket was raised slightly so one could recognize the face of the deceased from a distance. They were separated from each other by flowers or by closely placed miniature ficus trees.

The short ceremony for Mutti began in the rotunda. We stood around a plain four-wheel cart bearing the closed casket. Somewhere behind the walls, an organist intoned church hymns on a harmonium. Many years later, I recognized one of the melodies in my church choir singing. It was the *Sanctus* from Schubert's *Deutsche Messe* [German Mass].

After the musical interlude, we followed the funeral workers pushing the cart from the rotunda across the gravel paths to the prepared gravesite in a new part of the cemetery. Loose dirt had been heaped aside, forming a hill. We stood around the open pit, listening to the priest pray and sprinkle holy water. Then each of us in turn took a handful of dirt and flowers. Our last offering dropped with a thud onto the casket below.

On the way home, before we reached the tram, we stopped in a small restaurant. Vati and Adi had a beer and smoked cigarettes. I worked on a lemonade drink.

We could not afford a grave marker. A customary gravestone or sculpture was out of the question. In passing by surrounding graves in the cemetery during subsequent visits, we took note of the various markers. Some were massive headstones, others simple wrought-iron or wooden crosses. One or two graves were bare. Even to the very end, each grave reflected in some way the past status of the deceased.

Siegfried, who lived with his family in another part of town, was the middle son of my foster parents. He was known for his drawings and sketches. Some months after the funeral, he fashioned for his late mother's grave a wooden cross into which he carved the words "*Ich hatt einen Kameraden* [I once had a comrade]," the name of an old war song. Little did we know that cancer had already marked him. He died at age thirty-five and was buried in the same grave as Mutti around four years later in 1956. When he carved those words for her, he knew that he was writing his own obituary.

In 2018, during one of my last visits to Munich, I walked along that same path parallel to the Nordfriedhof cemetery wall. I no longer saw any war widows. Instead, I encountered other familiar images.

From behind the wall, reaching above it from the graves below, I recognized the same outstretched arm of a weather-worn marble cupid or the top of the same broken stone column representing a life cut short that I remembered seeing as a ten-year-old.

Could that have been the same old ivy, but with new tendrils, climbing along the wall, finding a way to the light outside the shaded burial grounds? *Memento mori* that had touched my sensibility two generations ago.

Vati

He was my mainstay, my anchor. Vati was a former SS man in his early fifties who agreed with Mutti to take me as a baby into his home, to take care of me when my birth mother could not be bothered with an infant. And he kept me even after Mutti died, when he could have easily turned me over to a municipal orphanage. Moreover, I am indebted to him for his teachings and for his efforts to bring some joy into my youthful existence, despite the difficult times all of us experienced.

I owe my fascination with nature to Vati. Through him, I became enchanted with flora. He taught me garden work, such as the proper watering and weeding of plants, and how to tell a sprouting flower from a weed.

He showed me how to plant seeds. With a garden dibble, he drew a narrow groove in the dirt parallel to a taut string attached at both ends of a bare vegetable or flower bed, dark earth still humid from his earlier shoveling. Carefully, one or two at a time, he dropped the grains in measured distances into the furrow, spreading a thin layer of dirt over it. To facilitate germination, he showed me how to gingerly level spurts of water from my can, making sure I did not flood the tiny groove.

Vati taught me the names of flowers: columbine, bleeding-heart, iris, stock, cosmos, hollyhock, marguerite, peony; of bushes: lilac, black elder, jasmine; and of trees: sour cherry, prune, plum, apple, pear. I learned to recognize the trees by their leaves, their bark, their fruit. I did get in trouble for plucking and eating unripe fruit, thereby diminishing our harvest. I couldn't wait until they were ripe. I always wanted to eat.

He taught me how to separate the tulip bulbs in the fall, how to cut off rhubarb twigs without pulling out the root, how to watch for the first signs of spring: The tiny yellow leaf points of *Schneeglöckchen* [snowdrop flowers] before they turned green, the tightly coiled blossom before it began to unfold its white helicopter-like propeller petals. He showed me how he prepared the winter garden, as we called it: Four boards formed a rectangular box around dirt, with a partitioned glass top raised at the head a couple of inches to let the sun enter at an angle.

By watching him, I observed how he was able to coax not only a wide variety of flowers but also bushes and trees from an unresponsive soil or after a hard winter freeze. He was especially skilled in grafting fruit trees, such as turning an ordinary plum into one producing Reine Claude Vertes or greengage (a type of green plum). His instruments consisted of a penknife, a special wax, and strips of linen. For this operation, he searched for a healthy mid-size branch in the tree, removed extraneous wood, reducing it to a small stump. He exposed and smoothed the cambium layer, made a deep vertical incision, inserted the scion, sealed it with the wax and wrapped the transplant tightly with cloth strips as if bandaging a wound. In spring, we could usually spot a sprout.

I also learned from him how to help myself to apples from

an absent neighbor's tree. "Why let good fruit go to waste?" Vati said as we clambered over the fence into another yard. Tiny pale-yellow apples hung in abundance from the branches of a tree that leaned over the back picket fence right next to the swiftly moving stream, the Eisbach, with only a foot-or-so-wide grass strip separating the fence from the water. My job was to remain on that strip. With a rake, I was to catch apples that had fallen into the stream after Vati had shaken the branches. With one hand, I held onto a fence picket, and with the other I maneuvered the rake while standing on the water-soaked grass. We collected the apples in a sack that Vati slung over his shoulder as we quickly retreated to our hut with the booty. The small apples were mealy but still a treat for us.

Thinking of Vati's opinion about the apples going to waste, I helped myself to the neighbor's hazelnuts. They grew unchecked and untrimmed on tall, spindly bushes and trees. I learned to recognize nuts getting ripe and started to root around the overgrown thickets. Squirrels and other critters didn't have a chance. I was like a semi-feral creature getting to the fruit before anyone else did.

Through Vati, I learned to appreciate a plant world beyond our Tivoli. I remember one or two beautiful afternoons spent at the *Botanischen Garten* [botanical garden] in Munich, where the two of us wandered among a multitude of flowers in bloom. We admired the exotic alpine plants growing in niches and cracks of man-made rock gardens. I was surprised to find that even the various grasses below the trees in the park-like areas were meticulously listed with their botanical names on markers.

Vati tried his best to find activities other than work for me. Whenever possible, he let me borrow his bike to ride along the narrow path in the Tivoli meadow bordering our yard. It was a black, very heavy, ancient men's bike. He taught me how to ride it. I managed to straddle it sideways by slipping my right leg through the metal triangle of the bike frame, placing my foot on that pedal. With my left foot on the left pedal, I would hurtle down the path trying to keep his bike in an upright position. I can't recall any serious mishaps.

In Germany, the first day of May is known as *Tag der Arbeit* [Labour Day]. I used to look forward to it, hoping for good weather. Vati often took Mutti when she felt well enough, Adi—if he was around—and me for a picnic in Grünwald, a forest area outside Munich.

We brought along sandwiches and something to drink, usually a bottle of beer for the men, and lemonade for Mutti and me. We took the tram to the end station and walked to find a suitable spot below a shady beech tree. I loved roaming around the greenery with the sun filtering through the canopy of the trees. I was always looking for unfamiliar weeds, plants, fruit, or nuts I had not yet discovered. I liked weeds because they were manifold; they even bloomed.

For a special treat, Vati took me swimming once in the Isar river, which flows through Munich. He bought me a bathing suit for the occasion, which made me feel rather special. With my new suit, I waded into the murky, shallow water of a little side stream and came out covered with mud.

Vati bought things for me whenever he could, sometimes beyond his means. During my last year in Tivoli in 1954, he bought me a new bicycle. Did he borrow the money for that purchase?

Later, when I was at the *Schwestern* [the Sisters] around 1957, he traveled once to Ankara, Turkey, for a two-month stay to visit an old friend, a distant relative of Ataturk, a past connection to his army days in World War I. During his absence, I was left at the Sisters, while the other resident girls were with their families to celebrate Christmas. Singing during Midnight Mass *"Ihr Kinderlein, kommet"* [Oh, come, little children] added a bit of irony as I was the only child kneeling in the pews among the black-hooded nuns.

Vati called his trip a sojourn in Anatolia. I received several postcards from him in which he wrote about his single duty to take care of me. He never forgot me.

What I Meant to Vati

I became his helper. I often had to help him gather *lumpen* [rags and trash]. In the postwar years, people did not have much to throw away, but we tried our luck anyway.

Our means of transportation for lumpen was a large two-wheeled cart. It stood about four feet tall, with wooden planks closing off the rear and the two sides. Vati stood with his back against it, took hold of the long, straight handles on either side, and with a big lift and a groan, tipped the whole thing toward his back to get started, then pulled, donkey-like, ahead. The cart was heavy, even without a load.

I trod next to him. We pulled slowly up the long incline, to the expensive part of town where the imposing apartment houses and old villas still stood in Bogenhausen, a part of

Munich that had been saved from the Allied bombing. With a bent back and a lowered head, he turned into the courtyards, where the trash bins stood hidden from the street.

I desperately wanted to hide because my schoolmates lived there. For some reason, the city authorities had assigned me to a school in that expensive part of town, even though we lived several miles away and in an entirely different neighborhood. I was afraid I would be spied from a window above, while Vati and I rummaged through their throwaways, loading them onto our wagon.

What were we looking for? Anything that could be eaten, worn, sold, or used in any form: An overlooked kohlrabi, part of an old pair of pants, wire, a piece of corrugated aluminum, bits of an old tool. And what we could not use, Vati tried to sell to the scrap metal dealer for pennies. But the pennies added up and helped feed us.

I Became Vati's Listener

From early on, I was a patient listener, a sounding board.

On rare occasions, Vati and Adi took me along when they wanted to meet friends at a café. The establishment was more like a pub with dark wooden benches and tables, coat racks at the entrance, calico curtains. The men ordered alcoholic drinks for themselves and a hot chocolate for me. They spent hours talking late into the night, while I sat quietly between them, slowly sipping my drink. As the evening wore on, I occasionally asked whether I could have another piece of cake. Thick, yellowish fog from the men's incessant cigarette smoking hung around our heads. The air was motionless, impenetrable. No one seemed to acknowledge that I was there. I was just a little girl wedged in among men who carried on noisy conversations.

I liked the tram ride home. That was the best part of the trip. After the ride, we had to walk home, about a mile, in whatever weather. But while we were in the tram, bathed in warmth and dull electric light, the gentle sways of the track movements gave me comfort. I felt secure in that enclosed box, looking out into the dark street, black apartment houses with only a light shining from a window here and there. It looked like the stage set of a theater play, with a twinkling star or the moon appearing briefly between chimneys above the roofs.

Often when Vati came home on his bicycle from his various odd jobs or from trips to town, I was waiting for him. He was tired, carrying impossibly large or awkward loads of whatever useful items he could find, or a large sack of our laundry. When we ran out of clean clothes, I helped Vati stuff a bag with soiled items, which he ferried to a dry-cleaner wash house. He paid to have the contents washed and spin-dried, known as *Trockenwäsche* [dry laundry]. Heaving that heavy, moist pack onto his bike rack, he pedaled home, where we sorted it, and I pinned it up on the clothesline for a final drying.

I usually met him a ways down the street. He rode on the bike lane, where I could see him from a distance. I would sit on one of the concrete kilometer markers nestled in the weeds next to the path. While I waited, I helped myself to a hunk of *Bauernbrot* [farmer's bread] and a beer bottle filled with water that I had brought along for sustenance. The beer bottles at that time still had a white porcelain stopper with a red rubber gasket connected to a thick metal clasp. It took all my strength and caution to open it and to snap it shut without getting my fingers caught in the rat-trap-like clasp.

Vati always seemed glad to see me. He got off his bike, and we talked on the way home. He was probably as lonely as I was. Who else was there to listen to him? Adi taciturn and preoccupied with caring for his domestic rabbits. Vati told me his stories, family history, and some war recollections. Due to my youth, much of that information passed me by for the moment, but not without leaving its mark to emerge clearer in my maturity.

What Vati Was

After Mutti's death in 1952, Vati changed completely. If before he suffered from periodic outbursts of rage and impatience, he was very quiet now. He performed his work in silence, a silence of endurance. He had to do his own cooking. His version of *Ersatz-Kaffee* (a mixture from various grains) was undrinkable. He taught himself to make pickled herring with onions and apple pieces. Herring was poor people's food at that time. (Today, I have to buy marinated herring from the deli.)

For years, Vati had stomach troubles. He used to come home bent over, holding his belly. It was time for an operation. When I visited him in the hospital, I saw him lying there, as white as his bed sheets, in a narrow, metal bed in an expansive, white-washed room with a high ceiling and tall windows. It was a beautiful, if antiseptic, room that dwarfed what was left of him, of his emaciated face and shrunken body. The hospital did not feed him intravenously. Perhaps it was not yet standard practice at that time. The body had to fight it out on its own.

He came home from the hospital much diminished. By then, I was already at the Catholic Sisters. According to their house rules, I could visit him in Tivoli just every other weekend, which allowed me to give him only scant help and comfort.

Vati was a skilled master gardener, a caring and generous family man who had become disenchanted with the Nazi culture. He had felt deceived. He had watched his family ruined, physically and mentally, by a war he had first supported.

His biggest concern was a life lived in vain. In October 1956, he wrote the following verse into my grammar school album:

Mit jedem Hauch entflieht ein Teil des Lebens,
Nichts beut Ersatz für das, was du verloren;
Drum suche früh ein würdig Ziel des Strebens;
Es ist nicht deine Schuld, daß du geboren,
Doch deine Schuld, wenn du gelebt vergebens.

Author's translation:
With every breath, a part of life disappears
No replacement for what you have lost.
Therefore, seek early a worthwhile goal in life.

It is not your fault that you were born,
But it is your fault if you have lived in vain.

Vati died six months after I emigrated to the United States. I never saw him again.

Adi

What was it like for a little girl to live with a foster brother who was two times her age?

Adi (short for Adolf) was born on April 20 (Hitler's birthday) in 1926. At age seventeen, he had been drafted into the German infantry and sent to fight the British in 1943. Almost immediately, he was shot during an attack and injured in his buttock. He ended up in Ireland (I believe) as a POW, where he rode Shetland ponies on a farm, enjoying what he called "the best years of my life."

Years later, I remember seeing a photo with crinkly edges yellowed by time. Adi is walking alone on a deserted country road, a gun slung loosely over his shoulder, an open jacket drooping from his skinny frame, a helmet dangling from a strip tied to his pants pocket, a vacant look on his face. It is an unlikely picture of a German soldier. It is a picture of a Caspar Milquetoast forced into arms.

Adjusting to the postwar years after his release was difficult for him. He could not keep a job for long, so he spent much time in his bachelor corner in Tivoli, occupying himself with the study of astronomy and ancient German sagas. He was a man of few words and checked emotions. But Adi always did as Vati told him. He never complained when called upon to chop wood for the stove or haul in coal briquettes, nor when major yard work was required, or the container in the outhouse needed to be emptied.

He liked raising rabbits. "They don't talk back," he said with a wink toward me. He was fastidious in cleaning out their stalls and in feeding them. Every so often, they ended up on our dinner table as delicious ragout. When it came time to slaughter one, I had strict orders to stay away. Sometime later, when I turned the corner of the veranda, the sight of a skinned rabbit chilled me: A naked pink corpse with its bony leg joints suspended upside down from a nail on the wall, a small pool of blood forming below. As sickening as I found the violence done to an animal, I had no trouble eating it for dinner. It all depended on my hunger pangs.

What Adi Did for Me

While I was at the Catholic Sisters, Adi appeared at the gate on several occasions holding a sack containing a loaf of fresh bread, a stick of butter, and a jar of strawberry jam. He handed it to me with the words, *"Zum Frühstück* [For breakfast]." He knew that our diet at the nuns was not abundant. He bought that treat for me with the few *Pfennige* [pennies] he had.

One Christmas Eve, he took me to Midnight Mass at St. Ludwigs Kirche, the neo-Romanesque church on Ludwigstrasse near the university in Munich. Deep snow everywhere. The two of us waded through drifts that reached my thighs, while we traced a shortcut through the park, the English Garden, to get there. I would have been lost without his unerring sense of direction in the still of a midnight-blue sky with stars blinking an eternity above the leafless treetops. We trudged along silently.

The church was filled to standing room. We squeezed in. The service had already begun. We joined the worshippers wrapped in coats, jackets, shawls, hats, gloves, and boots. Steam was rising from open mouths in the unheated stone church as we sang Christmas hymns in unison to organ accompaniment, sounds expressing devotion echoing from the walls. After that terrible war, we were all bound together on that Holy Night by hope, trust, and belief in a better future. Do people still go to church today in the same spirit?

On another occasion, Adi took me to the Münchner Marionettentheater am Gärtnerplatz. I was mesmerized by the marionettes, the play, the story, the fantasy displayed in the costumes and in the expressive motions of the puppets. I was transported to the world of make-believe.

Such memories return today when I see a print by J.J. Sempé[11] that shows a tiny boy, Nicolai, sitting by himself on a bench in the city park watching Guignol, the clown, in a makeshift puppet show, while his companions play hide-and-seek around the trees. I could be Nicolai, watching the show.

Adi even tried to teach me proper behavior. For example, he admonished me to treat food reverentially. "A loaf of bread must always rest right-side up, not on its belly," he insisted.

Another time, he gave me instructions about visiting his

---

[11] Jean-Jacques Sempé, French cartoonist (1932-2022).

friends in their new apartment. We had walked admiringly through the rooms until we arrived at their bedroom. Adi forbade me to enter: "One does not enter people's private quarters," he said, "even if invited." *Why*, I thought, until it dawned on me: *Oh, is that where they…?*

What I Did to Adi

Sitting next to him on our worn sofa that seemed to swallow me when I sat down, I couldn't avoid feeling every move Adi made, as he did mine.

Our sheer propinquity gave me an opportunity for leveling snide remarks at him about his personal hygiene. He absorbed my verbal darts with infinite calm and indulgence. Adi would mark the rare limit of his endurance by calling me under his breath *Fratz* [brat], which I eminently deserved as a twelve-year old.

I was unkind not only to him but also to his little Steiff-brand teddy bear. I tried to pull out his beady glass eyes. They were attached to a string that I could not remove, leaving the eyes hanging down his cheeks like falling teardrops. Why did I do that? Adi finally hid his bear from me for good.

Growing up, I did not appreciate his quiet, reserved demeanor, his saintly disposition. If I had his teddy bear today, I would take good care of it, as I would of Adi.

In 1990, at age sixty-four, Adi died unexpectedly in a hospital in Munich. In his coat pocket, the attending nurse found an open letter addressed to me with an unfinished sentence. I never saw the letter.

Tante Meta

When Mutti died in 1952, Vati realized that he could no longer run his household in Tivoli without help, especially since authorities questioned the ability of an old man—Vati was sixty-four by then—to take care of a ten-year-old girl who was not even formally adopted. He sent for his sister Meta, living in Thuringia in eastern Germany, asking her to come. Tante Meta became my foster aunt.

When I met her in Munich in 1952, I saw a tall, well-built lady in her sixties, who folded her gray-white hair into a braid, draping it like a thick cord across her nape, and pinning the tail end behind her right ear. She always dressed well in shirt-dresses or suits consisting of a wool skirt and a matching, fitted long-sleeved jacket with a blouse beneath.

In her youth in prewar Germany, Tante Meta had once ventured as far as Berlin, where she had spent her happiest days as a young woman, she said. She spoke longingly of ambling along Unter den Linden, the major boulevard in prewar days in Berlin, where the spring breeze flung about the sweet perfume of the linden blossoms. Years later, she married Konrad Krawietz, an engineer.

Tante Meta related to me how her happiness had been cut brutally short by a loud knock on their Berlin apartment door in the middle of the night around 1946. Jumping out of bed, Konrad, aiming for the door, called out, *"Wer ist da* [Who's there]?" Instead of an answer, he heard another hard rap. *"Aufmachen* [Open up]!" He did. Three dark-clad men entered with heavy footsteps. *"Krawietz, du kommst mit* [Krawietz, you are coming with us]!" they snarled, pushing him roughly.

"*Mach's schnell* [Hurry up]!" Out the door they went with him in tow, leaving Tante Meta to worry about him.

She never forgot those words: "*Krawietz, du kommst mit.*" It was the last time she saw him. She never heard from him. It was the time when the Soviet Union abducted countless professionals, transporting them to the Russian interior to work for them. She was forever faithful to his memory. Tante Meta never remarried.

My foster aunt had been raised in a strict Protestant household, where everyone had a task to perform, and no one was allowed to complain. She told me once of her sister, Ehrentraud, stirring a pot of soup on the stove during an unusually hot summer day. She stirred with a spoon in one hand, cradling her naked six-month-old baby boy in her arm, while holding only a loose diaper beneath his bottom with the other hand. Suddenly the baby's nature called, his clear fountain aiming straight for the soup pot. Too late to change course. Ehrentraud kept her cool, hoping no one had noticed. She served the soup at lunch. One of her sisters remarked: "This soup tastes different today," giving one of her brother's a chance to gibe her, "Just your imagination." It would have been inconceivable to waste that pot of soup, because during those times there was no food left to replace it.

For one year, after Mutti's death in 1952, Tante Meta kept Vati and me from drowning in our Tivoli misery by keeping the place clean as only she could. She was also an excellent cook. How was she able to cook and bake so well? How could she make such a delicious *Apfelkuchen* [apple cake]? She did not want me near her baking; she considered me clumsy. But for a treat for me, Tante Meta let me scrape the last bits of dough from the bowl. (I tried that treat many years later in the United States, when I handed a bowl with dough leftovers to my young stepson. He looked at me in astonishment. He was only interested in the finished product.)

After a while, Tante Meta desperately wanted *raus* [out], away from our bare-bones existence in Tivoli. Having successfully answered an advertisement for a housekeeper, she moved the two of us into a two-story house owned by a widower, Herrn Unruh. Vati had to learn to fend for himself now, while Tante Meta and I aimed for a new and better way of life.

His house was one of many row houses lining a busy street in a middle-level neighborhood. All houses were covered by the same postwar dirty gray stucco, gray slate pitched roofs, low gray concrete walls surrounded by a patch of grass. Some of the tall, colorful dahlias and asters peeking above the wall of his yard were tied together in bundles to keep them upright. It was fall.

Herr Unruh was a puffy-looking, practically bald, nearsighted gentleman in his late sixties, dressed every day in nondescript slacks, shirt, sagging sweater, and house slippers.

We had rules to follow, such as no toilet flushing between nine p.m. and seven a.m. The walls were thin. He did not wish to be disturbed. Utmost cleanliness was to reign at all times in all rooms. Beyond maintaining the house, Tante Meta was to cook and serve him his meals in the dining room, where he ate by himself at set times, while we were to eat in the kitchen nook. Above all, we were to pad about the house noiselessly.

One morning when I was late for school, I forgot to flush the toilet before I rushed off; there was only one in the house. During my absence, Herr Unruh must have paid a visit to the bathroom. Tante Meta told me later that the usually wordless gentleman had unleashed a thunderstorm of anger against her because of an unpleasant discovery he had made. I tried to visualize his tiny draw-string-purse mouth opening up suddenly in alarm, protesting, while my foster aunt retained her Prussian composure and dignity. He accused her of having left an unspeakable deposit in the toilet bowl. She defended herself by stating that it was not hers. He maintained, however, that no child could have left one that size. She would not tolerate his accusation. He would not accept her defense. There was only one way out of that standoff. We had to leave.

By then, Tante Meta had had enough—enough of managing our hut and me, enough of Herrn Unruh. She was also homesick for her Thuringia in East Germany.

From her, I had learned household tasks that I would not have learned otherwise. I admired her skill in cooking decent meals with the barest of ingredients. In hindsight, I appreciated her patience for putting up with my nascent teenage irascibility.

Most importantly, I am grateful to her for caring enough about my future to guide me to the next step of my growing up by opening the door to the Catholic Sisters. She was responsible for referring me to them and placing me on the waiting list in the St. Anna Heim, a private home for girls managed by the Niederbronner order of nuns. Perhaps I would qualify for one of only a couple of city-sponsored slots reserved for parentless girls from poor households, Tante Meta hoped. She strongly encouraged me to stop by the *Heim* [home] periodically, asking whether they had room for me. The Sisters accepted me in 1954.

Tante Meta and I wrote to each other on and off after her return to Thuringia. Years later, after I settled in the United States, I sometimes sent her a care package consisting of a few foodstuffs she wanted, such as coffee, chocolate, sugar, and flour, because they were hard to come by in Soviet-controlled East Germany. Preparing such a package was an exercise in endurance because I had to follow the strict requirements prescribed by the *Deutsche Demokratische Republik* [German Democratic Republic–DDR]. Every item had to be completely removed from its original packaging and poured, scooped, or placed in a plain brown paper bag and labeled according to content and weight.

With time, though, our correspondence diminished. Her life in the East had slowly improved, she wrote. And then, I never heard from her again.

In 1953, before she left, Tante Meta dedicated a short verse in my elementary school album, signing it with the words *Vergissmeinnicht* (after the forget-me-not flower). *Semper fidelis.*

Tante Anette

Tante Anette, Mutti's sister, was a confirmed bachelorette. Not by choice, but by conviction. I would see a pretty lady turn her sweet, round face with a peach-fuzz complexion and a pair of sparkling dark eyes toward me. Like a mother, she had words of wisdom and humor, endlessly giving of herself to family members, to children as well as to adults.

In the early 1920s, at Mutti's request, Vati had lent young Tante Anette tuition funds so she could attend the Kaufmännische Schule (a private business school). After graduating, she was able to support herself. She did so by becoming the most dedicated employee of the Seidl Bäckerei, the oldest bakery house in Munich. Tante Anette advanced to *Filialleiterin* [director], working her entire life at the main branch of the bakery in the original building at the Sendlinger Tor Platz, one of the busiest intersections in Munich. I remember her standing behind the counter in her snow-white work coat, her uniform. She manned that store as if it were her own.

Once, while I was visiting her during the 1950s, a lady customer walked into the bakery and immediately upbraided Tante Anette by waving a quarter-pound stick of butter she had purchased earlier in my foster aunt's face, loudly proclaiming that the water content in that piece was unacceptable. Tante Anette patiently explained to her that, first of all, the bakery bought butter from a dairy supplier and thus had no control over its consistency. Secondly, tiny water remnants were part of the churning process. And thirdly, Tante Anette would gladly exchange that piece for another one of choice, a suggestion that found immediate resonance with the shopper. My foster aunt bought back that piece of butter with her own money to balance her employer's books honestly.

Another time, Tante Anette overheard a young salesgirl in

the store tell a customer that the bakery did not have a certain type of bread available that day. The girl knew where the bread was stored; she was simply too lazy to retrieve it from the storage bin upstairs. Tante Anette shot out from behind the curtain that separated the storefront from the back room, declaring that that particular bread was indeed available. She then asked the girl to bring down the desired loaf. After the shopper left, my foster aunt gave the salesgirl a stern lecture.

Tante Anette treated me with utmost kindness when I visited. She let me sit at a small side table so I could watch her work. As a treat, she gave me a choice of pastry for which she reimbursed the store. It was always a holiday for me to be near her.

Sometimes she invited me to stay with her in her *Dienstwohnung* (an apartment her employer rented for certain employees as a courtesy). Livable abodes were still difficult to find so recently after the war's end. To enter that old dark building in the late 1940s and 1950s required a huge key that had to be inserted into the lock just right to get Sesame to open. The dampness and the smells from previous generations of living and cooking had penetrated the walls and hallways. (My sinuses can still sense them when I think of it.) Small half-rusted-out mailboxes were nailed along the wall in the vestibule where the paint started to form bubbles from the moisture. The residents' name labels on the boxes had been written in craggy handwriting, or they had been typed with a faded ribbon with a letter missing here or there.

Leading to the upper floors were dark wooden stairs with the middle part worn down to the width of a wafer, giving testimony to the many footsteps that had pressed down on them over the years. At each landing, a single light bulb shaded by a round metal disk was suspended from the ceiling. When I turned the switch, it was timed just so that no matter how quickly I ran up the stairs, the light went out before I reached the next level. All the renters, with their tired old bones, had to climb the last steps in the dark. Of course, no elevator.

Her quarters were on the third floor of that four-story apartment building. When I reached her door, another key with big teeth had to be worked into the lock. I entered a short, narrow, dark space that served as a coat rack and umbrella stand.

The apartment consisted of a living room with a kitchen nook and a bedroom. When the tall, narrow window in the living room was open, I felt deceptively close to the nearby church's twin towers with their onion-shaped cupolas. I thought I should be able to reach out and touch them. The church, called the *Frauenkirche* [the Church of Our Lady], is still Munich's landmark depicted on postcards today. The bong of the bells at mass time made the thick apartment walls vibrate. I slept on a little cot next to that window. To protect against the damp wall of that ancient building, Tante Anette had nailed a tapestry depicting a dark forest scene with an elk sporting a huge set of antlers. His open snout and raised neck in imitation of a roar used to frighten me.

A shaky gas stove in the kitchen was temperamental to light. My foster aunt knew its tricks and was able to get a sputtering flame up every time. A deep-bellied, enamel sink with an erratic drain hung from the wall next to the stove. A long-necked faucet with only cold water dripped into the rust spots of the drain. On a low stool stood a wide porcelain bowl with a matching jug. To wash ourselves, we heated water and poured it from the jug into the bowl. We grabbed a washcloth to rub us down.

The water closet lived up to its name. It was a tall, narrow space with a toilet too high for me to sit on comfortably; my legs dangled. The linoleum surrounding it was cracked. To flush the toilet, one pulled on a heavy porcelain grip shaped like an elongated teardrop. This handle was fastened to a chain hanging from a square metal box attached to the ceiling. I had to pull hard and often had to ask Tante Anette for help.

Today, this building, like others of that era, still stands, albeit *saniert* [remodeled]. Apartments in the heart of the historic downtown now rent for fabulous prices. Would Tante Anette recognize her old apartment today?

When I stayed with my aunt, she tried to take care of me as best as she could. But she was working full-time at the bakery, plus overtime when necessary, so she often coaxed other ladies in the building to take turns watching over me. They were either war widows or *Strohwitwen* [grass widows], a term applied to women who were temporarily without husbands. They were still expecting their men to return from the war. The apartment house was huge. I don't know how many different kindly ladies were corralled into babysitting me.

Tante Anette was the protector of the extended family of her sister, my foster mother. She put her freedom, her reputation, and her employment position at the bakery on the line when she hid her two older nephews returning from the Front. The American occupation forces sent MPs (military police) to conduct house searches to ferret out hiding fugitives and past participants in the war, people with a possible criminal record, who should be incarcerated and put on trial. Tante Anette's nephews were precisely the people being sought: Siegfried had served in the *Sturmabteilung* [SA] as a paratrooper in the Italian Dolomites, while Herbert in the SS had led an equestrian team into Warsaw, Poland.

My foster aunt was able to hide them in the warrens of her building until enough time had passed that the men could move on with clothes she provided and, of course, money. Through her courage and luck, the gamble was successful from the German standpoint. What gratitude did she receive from them? Her help was probably taken for granted.

In her young days in prewar Munich, Tante Anette was pursued by admirers. Engaged, she ended up pregnant. A marriage did not materialize. It was a time when women in that predicament tried to abort or, if unsuccessful, committed suicide. She used a knitting needle to rid herself of her unborn. Who helped her? Was she alone?

How did I hear about Tante Anette's ordeal? She confided in her sister, who told Vati, and Vati told me. As always, I was his last listening station. Mutti was often ill, and Adi kept to himself. Vati's older sons, Siegfried and Herbert, would only discuss the war when they spoke with their father. Tante Anette's experience was one of many hair-raising stories that dropped like seeds into my young being, sealed there only to germinate in later years to confront me with their brutality.

After I had immigrated to the United States in 1961, Tante Anette and I corresponded periodically. Later, when I was studying German literature in graduate school during the 1970s, she sent me the best books available.

I never hinted that I needed any material. Acting entirely on her own, she must have inquired in a Munich bookstore about what German students were studying. She probably shopped at Hugendubel at Marienplatz, a venerable Munich bookstore near her apartment house.

Her packages contained examples of classic and modern German literature, material on literary theory and criticism, such as W. Dilthey, R. Wellek, A. Warren, and J. Habermas, as well as information on literary hermeneutics, the theory and methodology of interpretation. She also included small boxes of beautiful art cards because she knew I liked art history.

Tante Anette died suddenly. The announcement reached me many months after her death. I had lost a parent.

Siegfried

Siegfried, my foster parents' middle son, did not live in Tivoli when I first met him in the early 1950s. He lived with his wife and young son in an apartment in town, a world away from us. Were we ever invited to their apartment?

Siegfried was the handsome one with his classically modeled head, blond hair, and clear-gray eyes that seized one with a steadfast look. He was tall, built like an athlete, truly the idealized version of the German soldier. Women would turn around to look at him, Adi said. While serving as a paratrooper of the SA in the Italian Dolomites, he was seriously injured during a landing. His lacerations became cancerous in subsequent years, a development that he kept from his closest relatives, with the exception of Adi who knew how to keep a secret.

Siegfried was an architect with an artistic bent, a talented draftsman who drew prize-winning sketches. After the war, he worked for the American occupation forces at the McGraw Kaserne, a former army barracks, in Munich. What his occupation and duties were during those years, we did not know, but it could well have involved drawing. He kept his silence about his work and about his illness, as he did about his war experiences.

January 6 is a legal holiday celebrated as Epiphany (*Heilig Drei Könige*) in Catholic Bavaria. On that day in 1956, Siegfrired's wife, Marlene, appeared at our garden gate with swollen red eyes, not saying a word. I opened it. She passed me on the way into our hut. I was a few steps behind her.

As I reached the open house door, I just caught the scene. Vati, wordlessly, threw the large kitchen knife he had been using against the wall, where the blade stuck in the wooden paneling. Marlene had just informed him that Siegfried had died that morning of cancer at age thirty-five.

We had to get ready for another funeral that would take place in the same cemetery where Mutti had been buried three and a half years earlier.

Another Funeral

Vati, Adi, and I were late to the ceremony. The huge doors of the funeral hall were locked. The service had already begun. What to do? The little square windows high up in the doors were too tall for us to reach. Adi lifted me up so I could see inside. I observed a large crowd of well-dressed mourners, standing in the rotunda, listening to a preacher's words. Catching my breath, I relayed the scene to Vati and Adi. "That couldn't be Siegfried's funeral," they said. Siegfried did not know that many people, or so we thought.

But this was the appointed hour for the service, so Adi knocked hard on the heavy entry portal until a clerk finally opened, eyeing us head to toe. He let us in after we explained ourselves. Everyone looked at us. We seemed out of place in our common clothes. We could not afford special funeral attire, so we wore our usual clothes with a simple black cloth band tied to the left upper arm of our coats. People's stares told us that we did not belong there, yet we were family.

After the last benediction, the clerk led us to the head of the line, as we followed the casket to the cemetery plot. The interment was a re-enactment of the one we had attended a few years earlier, with the excavated dirt unceremoniously heaped in a large pile next to the abyss. All of us stood around, taking turns dropping a handful of earth and a few flowers into the open pit. I cried profusely, mostly because of discomfort, unease, and alienation, and because Mutti had been buried there only three and a half years earlier. I was afraid to look into the tomb: Were her bones still visible—the coffin must be disintegrated by now? Standing apart unobtrusively from the mourners was a beautiful young woman. Adi informed me later that she was Siegfried's girlfriend.

Siegfried was an imposing figure. He didn't look like the rest of us. He didn't live like the rest of us. He didn't act like the rest of us. He seemed reserved and aloof, though not intentionally so. Was it because of his illness, his imminent death, or his war experiences? We shall never know. He kept his silence to the last.

The Metamorphosis of Herbert[12]

Herbert was the oldest son of my foster parents. He and his family lived with us in Tivoli for a while during the 1950s. But before I describe his early stay with us, I shall begin with an encounter between him and Vati, his father, who was seeking treatment at a dental clinic in Munich in 1959. Vati recounted to me their meeting.

Herbert made his way quickly along the hallways in the student dental clinic, sneaking into the room where Vati was reclining in a dental chair, mouth propped open by a clamp, cotton pads filling the inside of his cheeks and lower mouth, a student holding the drill at the ready. Herbert had propitiously planned that moment to ask his father for money. Vati, with a helpless squawk, pointed one arm embarrassed and annoyed toward the coat rack on the wall holding his jacket from which Herbert fished out some bills. Off he went until next time. That was Herbert, shiftless,

[12] First published with some changes in the Chaffin Journal (2019): 7-9.

penniless, forty years old, borrowing from his poor, almost seventy-year-old, father who had to go to a dental school for free tooth repairs.

Going back about fifteen years earlier, Herbert had been an imposing figure in his tall and powerful frame, noble face, ramrod posture, and studied body movements, I was told. His pictures show him in a three-quarter profile in his officer's SS uniform, that symbolic hat pulled deep down his high forehead, the *Eiserne Kreuz* [Iron Cross] pinned to his jacket, jodhpurs riding pants, leather knee-high boots. Did his hands behind his back hold a riding crop?

Sometime after the war, a man called for Herbert at the fence gate of our hut in Tivoli. After a long trek around the country, he finally located Herbert. Erich Hochstetter was his name. We bade him inside, and the two met.

Standing face to face, Erich at first slowly, then more and more passionately, explained the circumstances under which they had met. Herbert had been the leader of a German equestrian platoon invading Hungary during the early 1940s. Erich had been one of the troops. Herbert had saved his life during a deadly ambush. Erich kept talking about the battle, while Herbert stood staring straight ahead, silently, no muscle in his face belying his emotions. Not seeming to get through to him, Erich fell to his knees. Near sobbing, he kept repeating: "You saved my life!—Don't you remember?" To no avail. Herbert could not be moved. Stifling his sobs, Erich finally gave up. He stood up and, bending over slowly, walked out, inconsolable. He and Herbert were the sole survivors of that platoon.

After the visitor left, I witnessed a telling moment in a conversation that revealed its meaning to me only with time: Vati had turned to Herbert, looking him straight in the eye while pointing his finger at him, saying, "But you were in Warsaw," implying that Herbert had been present at the Warsaw Ghetto massacre.

One day during the early 1950s, Herbert, his wife, Helene, and their two teenage children from her previous marriage, Robert and Liliane, showed up for an indefinite stay with us in Tivoli, because they had run out of money. Helene was a beautiful woman: Tall, blond, well-built, with classic features. Herbert had fought hard to take her away from her first husband. In my presence, he showed Vati a picture of her nude languishing in a small wooden rowboat, a transfixing sight to an eight-year-old girl.

When they arrived in Tivoli, Helene strode into our tiny two-room hut erect and purposeful, dressed tastefully, showing a definite sense of elegance and fashion despite their strained finances. Looking around over her shoulder, taking in the milieu in which she found herself now, she exclaimed, "It smells of poverty." The family stayed nevertheless. Vati, having given up most of our bedroom to them, relegated Mutti and me to a corner there, while he slept on the sagging couch in the kitchen/living room.

One evening, we children were sitting by candlelight, our only means of light as we had run out of kerosene for our lamp. Left alone, Robert, Liliane, and I made a bit of a game of the dripping candle wax. We carefully peeled the glistening soft wax drops off the sides of two white candles before they hardened. We slowly chewed and swallowed it. We went to bed.

Returning home, Herbert walked into the dark bedroom with a flashlight. We woke instantly. "Who removed the candle wax?!" he intoned. The air felt suddenly charged, like in an interrogation chamber. The three of us raised our arms out of the bed covers. What was our crime—eating candle wax? His answer was waiting for us.

He stood there in his six-foot frame, with muscles like one who had taken boxing lessons in his early life, loosely holding part of a rubber car tire tread by his side. Car tires at that time came in two parts, like those of bicycles: A smooth inner tube and a hard outer tread. He carried a half-circle of tread reaching from his lowered arm to his calves. A colossus eyeing us.

Advancing slowly toward Robert's bed, he lifted his cover, commanding him to turn over. Raising the tire tread with both hands over his head, he brought it down with all his might onto Robert's rear. He repeated the salvos mercilessly to his son's screams.

Liliane knew she would be next, and she was. The thwacking stopped. The screaming turned into nonstop wailing.

Herbert's hard steps approached my bed. He stared down at me silently for what seemed an eternity. I was in rigor mortis, my fingers clawed around the top of the bed cover pulled right up to my mouth. Did he expect me to turn over voluntarily? I held fast; so did his eyes. I held my breath. All of a sudden, his fist released the weapon. It slid slowly from his hand to the floor. He seemed spent. Did he spare me because I was not one of his children? I was his unofficially adopted foster sister.

Years later, after emigrating to the United States, I paid Herbert a visit in 1964 on a rare return to Tivoli. By then, the city had declared our hut condemned, with signs posted on the door and outside walls. But Herbert still lived there defiantly, alone now, in abysmal conditions. A faux Persian carpet tacked on one wall, sullied cracked and chipped dishes about, in the corner a bowl filled with fetid water and a rag. I had come to help.

Night fell. He paced about the tiny room. I sat on a worn-out couch between protruding springs, a rough-hewn kitchen table between us. We were making small-talk.

Herbert became animated. I started to feel uncomfortable under his warming persona. It was too late to leave. It was dark. There was no phone, no means of transportation nearby, no immediate neighbors. Our hut was at the end of a meadow near the English Garden, a public park at the edge of town. The nearest tram station was almost a mile away. I felt trapped.

He paced around the confined space of the cramped kitchen. Pearls of sweat were forming on his forehead. I started to fear him. I suddenly remembered incidental remarks from the past. He was thought of as a man "who had to have a woman every so often." I tried to cool the conversation by segueing into an intellectual topic that I thought would interest him: Nietzsche. I had vaguely heard him discoursing about that topic in family arguments.

I knew nothing about Nietzsche beyond the name, but in my desperation, I kept Herbert talking by proffering questions he seemed quite willing to expound upon. I stretched my imagination to the point where I was sweating, too, scared to death, smelling the advances of a rape as he leaned closer to me across the table, a metallic gleam in his eyes. I thought of ducking suddenly below the table and escaping between his spread legs. But could I extricate myself from the grip of a charged male?

Dead tired, yet alert in fear, I somehow managed to keep him talking through the night, his speech becoming more and more a soliloquy, while never letting me out of his eyesight.

Did I see daybreak creeping in alongside the window? Did Herbert's pace slack?

In slow motion, I raised myself from the couch. Like prey caught in a cat's laser vision, I watched his every move while I squeezed along the wall in carefully measured inches, then out of the hut, numb in spirit, and in a last leap of desperation, I ran and stumbled on borrowed energy through the yard, out of the garden gate, through the meadow the mile to the tram station, almost collapsing in exhaustion and relief, as I clambered into the streetcar, helped up by a passenger, my legs and shoes covered with clumps of dirt, weeds, and wild flowers from the dewy meadow. Did he try to follow me? I don't know; I never looked back. I had only a few coins on me to pay for my tram fare.

Much later, I heard that Herbert had met his end, a casualty of old age, in a care home for men in Munich.

Traute's Role in Tivoli

Today, I feel that I was a cuckoo's egg placed there by my birth mother, although my foster family never treated me as such. Instead, they showed me kindness if not indulgence. I am sure I ate more than my share of their daily bread.

I tried to help with household and yard chores. And although I suffered through a number of Vati's fiery outbursts, before Mutti's death softened him and his illness weakened him, I must have complicated the family's life with my periodic disobedience and usual growing pains.

Difficulties

But I had problems of my own to solve. Despite Mutti's efforts to keep me neat and clean when she was still well enough, my personal hygiene suffered. One time, I developed a tooth abscess. Swelling and pain let me open my mouth with only a mere crack. In the dentist's office, a handsome dentist couple, who looked intimidating to me in their crisp white uniforms, took one look at me and encouraged me to brush my teeth more often.

I tried to keep clean and dry during rains on the two- to three-mile walk to school with cars hitting the puddles as they made their turns. I still recall the old Volkswagens with their funny turn signals, little metal sticks that flipped out from either side window at the driver's command—no automatic lights yet.

I tried to keep fear at bay while walking home from school in the dark during winter. I had to decide which path to take: Should I use the sidewalk next to the street with dim streetlights, where an occasional car passed by at that hour, but where I would be noticed and possibly become vulnerable to an attack? Or should I hurry through the pitch-dark Tivoli meadow, sight unseen?

Fear gripped me, too, at home, because I was often left alone in the hut at night. Vati was working as a night watchman at some establishment. And who knows where Adi was? He didn't tell us. During storms, I shuddered when the wind howled through the trees, battering the roof and the walls with broken branches, when heavy rains blinded the windows.

I tried to fend off loneliness and melancholy. I entertained myself by watching nature, by writing poems, and by daydreaming.

What I missed were friends, toys, and books. My school textbook was the only book I had. The school lacked a library. I was not aware at the time that the city library offered free borrowing privileges. The branch was located several miles away.

Three-Way Tension in My Life

At certain times, I faced the forces of parents, school, and church colliding. The three entities had little, if anything, in common, yet I had to navigate between and among them.

Tivoli was a world of its own with house rules to heed. But Tivoli was relevant. I ate and slept there. It was home.

School was a closed environment with teachers' instructions to observe. I thought their demands were excessive. I could not see that school improved our daily lives.

The Catholic Church, with its doctrines, seemed remote, because I did not understand the basis for the decrees. The mysticism of the Latin mass, the pageantry, and the music felt remote, too, but in a different way; they let me escape the ordinary to a higher realm.

These tensions among parents, school, and church are mirrored in my celebration of First Communion.

Breaking Bread

I had been baptized Catholic at the birthing section of the municipal hospital in Munich. Both Vati and Tante Meta, who was living with us during the time of my First Communion in 1952, were Protestants from Prussia. I was a Catholic living in a Protestant household.

Not that Vati and Tante Meta were close observers of their religion, but they were dead-set against anything having to do with the Catholic Church. Growing up, I often heard Vati rant and rave about the "damned Catholics," whom he also called "charlatans," while a different spirit prevailed at school.

Our fourth-grade class was preparing for our First Communion with special lessons about the meaning of "Breaking Bread with the Lord." To that end, we had to follow strict protocol in our attire for the forthcoming church ceremony. Our dress was the only thing that really mattered to us ten-year-olds.

Preparations for that event were an expensive proposition for at least some of the parents during those early postwar years. The theme for that Sunday was "white." A white dress of a certain length with long sleeves and a small collar, stockings and shoes to match, a garland of white fabric flowers in the hair, adorned with specks of green leaves. Thus was the custom. Each child was to carry a white candle, one-and-a-half feet tall and one inch in diameter. Decorated with gold or silver ecclesiastic symbols, the candle was tucked into a tightly pleated paper rosette, a *bobèche* [candle ring], designed to catch the melting wax tears during the ceremony. There were stores, of course, catering to these specific requirements.

My family could ill afford such finery. My foster father suggested that if these "clowns" [*Hanswursten*] at church demanded all of that, they should have furnished it. He meant it, too, so I had to take the next step myself.

I knocked at the parish door, hoping for help from the monsignor. Looking at me in surprise through a half-open door and listening to my story, he offered that dresses were occasionally donated to the church after the event, because, like wedding gowns, they were worn only once. He would inquire.

But first, I had to pass a test. He asked whether I had been a good girl, whether I had been attending Sunday church services faithfully, and whether my foster people were good Catholics. "They are Protestants," I answered without elaborating. "We'll see what we can do," he called out by way of goodbye.

Thanks to him, I ended up with a loaned dress that was a bit short and snug, and cotton stockings that were too long, but both would do. Most of the other needed items came together somehow just in time for the big day.

The Catholic Church, famous for its 2,000-year tradition,

heightened the pageantry that Sunday morning. Imposing organ music resounded from the thick stone walls of the Gothic revival church, St. Johann Baptist (if my memory serves me correctly), with its faded, gilded plaster-of-Paris figurines. A white cloud of little girls was kneeling in the first rows of carved, dark wooden benches. Behind them sat the parents mostly dressed in their best black suits, the women in hats adorned with veils. Our tall candles flickered slowly. Incense, spilling from ornate vessels, swung in rhythm by the acolytes, enveloped the pews—mesmerizing sounds, smells, and sights.

Being Protestants, Vati and Tante Meta asked Adi, who was baptized Catholic, to accompany me to church. Vati must have notified my birth mother, and she came for the event, meeting Adi and me at the church.

She was thirty-three years old and looked like a movie star to me. She stood out from the other dark-suited parents in her tailored bright yellow cloth coat with a brown velvet collar and cuffs. The breeze turned up a corner of her coat, exposing brown satin lining. She wore color-matched gloves, suede high heels, and a rakish hat with a plume, so the photo of that day showed.

Next to her in the picture stood Adi, who had slipped out of his lair earlier than usual that day to accompany me, upholding the Tivoli family honor. He wore a typical postwar poor man's herringbone suit. His tilted hat covered a swollen cheek resulting from a bee sting the previous day when he had helped Vati trim an overgrown tree in the yard that was hiding a swarm of bees. Propped up between my mother and

Adi, I donned a self-conscious smile, aware of my ill-fitting dress and stockings that were beginning to obey laws of gravity and motion.

Each family had its own plans for the rest of the day. Adi left us to meet friends in town. Then a school acquaintance and her mother approached my mother and me, suggesting that we have lunch together. I knew, of course, that my foster parents were preparing a special meal at home for the occasion. I was weighing both options. Contacting my family about our new plan was impractical because we lived several miles from church, with limited public transportation. We had no telephone.

I was torn between having to choose between a rare opportunity of lunching in a restaurant, one that had long lace curtains inside and blue or pink hydrangeas outside, and a meal at home in an overcrowded tiny room steamed up from cooking. I would have to listen once more to my foster family rail against the extravagant "circus" we little individuals had been subjected to that day in church. And I would have to help with the cleanup later. Eating out won.

After our restaurant lunch, my birth mother and I arrived in Tivoli a couple of hours later. Now we had to admit that we had already eaten. The dam broke. My foster parents had been waiting for us all that time while keeping the food warm. Vati roared. Tante Meta bit her lip, wiping her hands on her kitchen apron. My mother, the glamour girl, looked around to see how quickly she could extricate herself from this potentially dangerous situation and from such shabby surroundings. I shivered in my little white dress.

Then, like a bat out of hell, a big flat hand struck my face. Was it hard slaps on each cheek or just on one, I don't recall. "That'll teach you," bellowed my foster father.

My mother and I had snubbed the old folks' invitation to share the table with them. Instead, the two of us had chosen to "break bread" with strangers in a public place.

And, not to forget, we had ignored the foster parents' preparatory efforts. A week before, Tante Meta had begun with the arduous grocery shopping. That meant walking a good mile to the nearest tram station, and at the end of the ride walking to different stores: One for dairy products, another for meat, a third for produce, and so on. Finally, laden with bags and bulging shopping nets, she had to repeat the tram ride and the long walk home.

Nor were the cooking and baking easy with an old coal-and-wood-burning stove in our tiny kitchen, without running water, without electricity. Our special meal that Sunday was to have been a feast.

Vati's angry reaction against my flagrant disrespect of their labor was salvo number one.

Salvo number two followed the next day at school. Several needy pupils, I among them, had received a cash donation a few days earlier to be used by our parents to commemorate that Sunday in a special way.

The following Monday, we children had to report how these funds had been spent. Standing in front of the class one by one, my compatriots told of a trip taken to one of the lakes in the nearby Alps, or a visit to the botanical garden, or to a theater performance in town.

I was last. Still smarting from salvo number one, I simply said, "The money went for food." Everyone looked at me in silence. After our teacher found her voice again, she sputtered, "Just for food?" Indeed, was it not used for "breaking bread?"

Our Neighbors: The Old Lady Next Door

Our place seemed lonely, because the few neighbors who permanently lived in Tivoli seldom, if ever, came to visit. For the others, it was not uncommon to be absent for months at a time.

But across the fence, I caught glimpses here and there of a lady living right next to us. She waded silently through her magical flower garden: Prize-winning tulips, various types of narcissus, rare lilies, huge stalks of gladioli, asters and dahlias with multicolored flower petals arranged symmetrically in huge disks, grand roses of every kind and size, including climbers, according to season.

Was she a war widow? She was of undetermined old age. Her lips seemed folded inward. Her penetrating eyes stood out from her puffy face surrounded by black-gray hair pulled tightly into a small doughnut-shaped bun. A homespun calico dress and bibbed apron wrapped her bulky body. Threadbare sandals covered with yard dirt covered her feet. She never spoke. We never learned her name.

More than once, I felt her Medusa eyes lock into mine through the fence pickets. "Warning! Stay away from my flowers," they seemed to shout. Yet, I so wanted to be near her flowers, to sit among them, to look at them, to possibly even touch them carefully and in wonder. I was fascinated by their beauty, by their kaleidoscopic colors, by their exotic forms, by the way their faces turned toward the sun. I thought I had spied a magic land through the paling. Out of fear, I stayed on my side of the fence.

But I could not control our vagabond cats trespassing in the old lady's yard. They paid a price. I had to watch as one cat after another first disappeared for days, then returned sick, dying a slow grim death of powerful poisoning. In their agony, they stretched their stiffened limbs to the extreme, sometimes pushing straight through the solid-weave cat basket positioned near the stove in the kitchen. Each time one died, I fashioned a cross with two twigs and placed it on the graves I had dug for them in a corner of the yard.

The Werners

The Werners, who lived several garden plots away from us, were of a different sensibility. Herr Werner was a short, spindly gentleman in his fifties, who worked at the Tivoli mill in some capacity. He could barely keep his pants from sliding down his narrow hips. Olive skin with a shock of graying hair slicked back, and sharp, dark eyes crowned by a bushy, unruly arc of eyebrows framed his spiky cheekbones and hollow cheeks. He led the family roost with a commanding voice, or was it just blustering? I was not sure.

But I was sure about Frau Werner, a large woman of the same age as her husband. She wore a perennial long-suffering expression in her round face with a mere trace of eyebrows and early graying, thin hair cut to medium length, combed back where it would not stay. A kitchen apron enveloped her body, her varicose-veined legs stuck permanently in felt slippers with holes cut out, revealing huge bunions.

Frau Werner was a superior cook and baker. Her wafer-thin, unadorned star-shaped butter cookies were made with real butter, a rarity during the early postwar years. Weeks ahead of Christmas, she baked them by the dozen and packed them away in cardboard boxes, hiding them from marauding family members or other critters. How the sweet cookie perfume failed to give away their secret hiding places was a mystery to me.

Angela, their young daughter, was a willful child of my age, about nine at the time. She was very alert and clever, and undisciplined, while being carefully watched over and coddled by her family. She was physically and mentally premature. Angela suffered from a severe speech impediment, war-related, her family insisted. She could emit only approximate sounds that consisted mostly of vowels and mangled consonants. Angela had her own speech pattern that I understood and learned to mimic, to her parents' consternation. Angela and I got along well.

The Werners tolerated my frequent presence on account of my friendship with Angela, giving me ample opportunity to observe their household and its denizens. Angela's older sister, Liese, was a pretty lady in her twenties with willowy red hair. She often sat on a chair by the window with her toes clamped onto a rung of a stool opposite her, a hand mirror pressed unsteadily between her knees, removing unwanted facial protrusions with tweezers, making grimaces in the process that I thought funny.

The Werners embodied utmost integrity and kindness. They fiercely protected their own, yet were quite willing to share their last piece of food with strangers in need. They put up with my presence at all times, even during their frequent family rows when proper comportment on my part demanded that I leave immediately. Herr Werner would straighten himself up to confront Frau Werner, who withstood him with grace and patience. It was never clear to me why they argued because I could not make out his thunderous words accompanied by wild gestures. No blows were ever exchanged. It was probably all wind.

In accepting me into her family, Frau Werner shared her precious Christmas cookies and included me in occasional candy purchases for Angela at the street corner kiosk about a mile from us.

I was her daughter's only companion, as she was mine. We were the only children in that neighborhood.

Chapter III: A Christmas in Tivoli[13]

A week before Christmas, Vati brought into the kitchen a four-foot spruce he had just cut from somewhere and stood it up on a stand he had made by nailing two wooden slats together crosswise, cutting out a round opening in the middle to wedge in the tree. It smelled fresh of forest with melted frost droplets still glistening on its branches.

He placed it in the corner next to the buffet and began decorating it with apples, oranges, and walnuts. Vati took thin copper wire he had cut into five-inch lengths and pushed one through the center of each fruit, bending the protruding end so that the fruit held. He shaped the upper extension into a hook to hang the apples and oranges onto the tree branches. He tried the same method with the walnuts with somewhat less success because of their hard shells.

Tante Meta and I helped by wiring four-inch-tall white candles to the ends of the branches. We did not have little candle holders that came with clip-on snaps for that purpose.

---

[13] First published in the Freshwater Literary Journal (2022): 59-60.

Fruit and candles were all we had for decorations. I thought our tree was rather festive once the candles were burning, warming the resiny fruity air.

With his sonorous bass voice Vati, the old WWI and WWII warrior, slowly intoned, *"Es Ist Ein Ros' Entsprungen* [Lo, How a Rose E'er Blooming]," a melody that still resonates deeply with me today. He also played the harmonica quite well. Adi chimed in with more songs of the season. Vati and Tante Meta knew all the verses of the old songs by heart, while I could only hum along after the first one. The blending of voices rendered our little hut almost reverential, conjuring in my mind thoughts of Christmas angels like those depicted on Advent chocolates and candy wrappers.

We munched on some cookies or a piece of *Guglhopf,* a type of pound cake, quite tasty when Tante Meta baked it. Maybe we even had a cup of real coffee. The men drank beer and stronger stuff that I don't recall.

The treats must have reminded Vati of his youth in Thuringia. In telling his stories, his voice became more and more gravelly with drinking as he segued into his war experiences.

He told of the time he was riding his bike along a country road in the east in 1944 when he was approached by a Polish man who stopped him, motioning to turn over the bike to him with the few German words: *"Das ist mein. Jetzt kannst Du laufen* [It's my bike. Now it's your turn to walk]." Vati thought it best to do as told, because he was on Polish territory, land that had been traded back and forth between Germany and Russia.

Adi then followed with his story of being in the German infantry in 1943. It was Christmas Eve. The soldiers decided to fry a stack of pancakes for supper when their guard came running in, warning of an approaching enemy patrol. They hurried out of the tents and hid in the surrounding forest. When it was quiet again, they returned. The pancakes had gone missing. The Brits had absconded with them. In exchange, they had left a box of cigarettes with a thank-you note and a Merry Christmas wish.

With thoughts of war on their minds, Vati and Adi shifted to singing war-time pop songs like "Lili Marleen."

The air in our hut had thickened with wafts of cigarette smoke and fumes of alcohol. The men's pitch rose, arms started to gesticulate. There was nothing stopping Vati now as he worked up a sweat ranting and raving about the war, about what would have been, could have been, should have been.

The tone in our kitchen started to get serious. Adi tried to steady Vati as he lurched toward him wielding a large kitchen knife. When Adi caused him to drop it, Vati in his rage lunged for the few dishes we had, smashing every plate, bowl, and glass within reach to smithereens. Tante Meta and I were crouching in a corner by the stove trying to avoid the shards raining off the wall.

Vati's thunderous stream of consciousness began to dissolve into grunts. He was done. He lumbered, head bent, shoulders sagging, toward his bed, a broken man acknowledging his entire family destroyed by war and self-destructed by disappointment, anger, and alcohol.

The burning candle wicks on the Christmas tree began to spat, sizzle, and crackle as they neared the end of their life, warm melting wax dripping from the branches. It was time to extinguish what was left of them. The fruity tree decorations, too, were on the wane, the apples dropping in pieces, the oranges into mush on the floor. Even the hardy walnuts were showing the first dark-brown spot of decay.

Another Christmas had passed with thoughts of past Christmases ghosting about.

Chapter IV: Elementary School

Former President Nixon once said that it all starts in school, the inequities, that is. I say it all starts in Kindergarten.

Today, I can still smell the vinegary soup of cabbage, or was it potato, ladled into our individual bowls or cups as we were waiting in a long line in front of an administration building in the late 1940s. "Did you get more soup than I did?" we questioned, as we peeked into each other's dish. "Is my piece of bread bigger than yours?" Or, "Why do you get to nap on a cot, while some of us have to sit in chairs resting our heads on the play table due to the usual lack of cots?" Who were the favored ones? Who decided that?

Only later in the long line for polio vaccination were no favorites. Everyone received the same two scratches on the skin. The button-like scar is still visible on my upper right arm.

My Path to Elementary School

We lived about two to three miles from school. Along the way, I crossed the bridge spanning the Isar river. On a hill on the right, I took in the tower and its double-onion-shaped verdigris cupola of the St. Georg *Kirche* [church] that reached above the trees hiding the small, well-maintained cemetery. Today, one can find there the graves of the German author Erich Kästner and the filmmaker Rainer Werner Fassbinder.

Nearby in the state park was the Schlittenberg (aptly named sled hill). In winter, I had trouble controlling my sled, because the snowy slope had turned to bumpy ice by the many children's sleighs that had skidded and raced down before me.

A steep incline led up to the school grounds. Occasionally, on the last leg of my journey, I passed one of my schoolmates accompanying our teacher, a large lady who carried a huge leather briefcase with outside pockets held together with two wide leather straps wound around them.

It was an honor to be allowed to carry her bag up that hill. I was not one of the chosen. In retrospect, I am rather glad, because her bag seemed far too heavy for one of us little girls to schlepp. I do remember that particular teacher's fondness of the hymn *"Näher mein Gott, zu Dir"* [Nearer my God to Thee], which she used to sing to us periodically. To this day, I associate that song with her, with ambivalent feelings.

The Place

Gebeleschule was named after the teacher Joseph Gebele (1853-1910). Built in 1911, the school encompassed a four-story building, a type of neo-baroque style, with a red tile roof and dormers. The outside walls showed dark gray stucco dirtied from years of neglect during the war years. The building stood by itself like a somber behemoth of stone surrounded by weedy stretches of lawn and some mature trees.

Today, the school appears rather inviting with its fresh coat of light-colored paint and well-kept entry paths and lawns.

The city education department assigned me to this school in the upscale neighborhood, called Bogenhausen. A few years later, I was transferred to a school in another section of town. It was as if the city did not know where to place me.

We lived on the edge of town with few neighbors and even fewer children. I was separated, then, from my classmates, not only geographically but also economically, because no one in my class lived anywhere near me.

The only one close to home was Angela, the Werners' daughter with the speech problem, but her parents kept her away from school. That meant that I had no classmates to walk with, to converse with, to play with, nor to share school assignments.

After school, all students quickly dispersed and disappeared into their respective neighborhoods, a universe removed from mine.

I sought friendship, yet I feared it. I wanted to ask my classmates to come and see me. But could I really invite someone into our hut in Tivoli? What would a girlfriend think of our circumstances? I knew where most of them lived. I passed by their houses and villas on my way to school. I was simply ashamed.

The Classroom Bearing Witness

A small crucifix hung on the white-washed wall. Students'

desks consisted of a heavy, dark wooden table with a bench screwed to the floor.

Pitiless regimentation. Respect for hierarchy.

The teachers were all old women with the exception of our religious studies teacher, a priest borrowed from the parish. After hearing the class bell, we followed orders, a routine so accurately described in *Les Années* [The Years] by Annie Ernaux, the French novelist and 2022 Nobel Prize winner. Strict discipline was not unique, then, to Germany. Praise was sparse.

Extra-curricular activities as we know them today were non-existent. We did have instruction in physical education, but the hour was regimented like all school subjects. What did we do during recess? I don't recall, except that it did not seem long enough for me to get to know other students well.

Our Studies

In religious studies, we did not read the Bible. We used a booklet that concentrated on the Roman Catholic Church calendar, the holidays, the rituals, and the rules, such as no meat consumption on Fridays. Rote learning. Beyond the usual basic general topics, we covered nature studies that led to occasional excursions to the nearby moraines left from melting prehistoric glaciers. I diverted myself from these sleep-inducing trip narrations by spying a pretty purple thistle along the way or a swaying butterfly, inattention that was reflected later in my grades.

From the German language class, I especially remember learning a typeface, a particular calligraphy, called *Fraktur* script. Instead of round letters, each such letter is a reassemblage of broken parts, giving the printed page a somewhat crowded, less-smooth look. I did not appreciate the effort then, but this skill allowed me to read older printed versions of German literature many years later in college classes in the United States. *Fraktur* is no longer part of today's school curriculum in Germany.

We also, very briefly, studied *Sütterlin*, a craggy, older version of German handwriting dating to 1911, forbidden by the Nazis in 1941, and replaced by the Latin alphabet writing. *Sütterlin* is no longer taught, either. I can still read it, although slowly.

Certain writing assignments had to be done in India ink. The nib of a steel point pen of a particular size had to be inserted into the pen holder and dipped into the ink pot just so. In writing, one had to learn not to press too hard, or it would leave a fat spot of black ink on the page that could not be erased; nor too lightly, or it would leave pen scratch marks, a task I never mastered, and one I would find difficult to accomplish satisfactorily even today.

Sewing class was fearsome for me. We used the old treadle sewing machines. I thought they were huge black beasts. One had to rock the footrest in a steady rhythm to keep the needle humming. I could never get the right tempo, that is, keeping it even. Scared, I stopped. The needle broke off, and the thread in the spool knotted up. I never managed the proper pearl stitch in the French-cuff samples we had to prepare.

As much as I disliked sewing then, I did keep the wooden accordion-style sewing basket containing basic essentials, namely various sizes of needles, pins, threads, and measuring tape. I even brought it with me from Munich when I emigrated to the United States in 1961. I still use it today.

Hidden in the bottom of the basket is a *Pilz* (a piece of wood shaped like a big mushroom) for mending socks. If a *Pilz* was not available, one had to use a lightbulb. One would spread out the defective part over the rounded head of the *Pilz* in order to smoothly weave the hole shut without leaving a ridge that would chafe the wearer's foot later. Does anyone still mend socks today?

I also still have an old German *Nadeleinfädler* [needle threader] for sewing by hand. It is a sliver of diamond-shaped foil with a thin wire loop attached at the end. One has to feed the thread through its loop, which is pliable enough to push the pointed end containing the thread through the needle opening. One can then easily pull the thread through.

Who would use such a tool? A seamstress with poor eyesight who has trouble threading a needle?

Were those instruments part and parcel of our preparation for life? Why do I still keep the wooden *Pilz* for mending socks? Why do I still have a *Nadeleinfädler?* Are they proof of hard lessons learned in early school days?

The People: Portraits of the Teachers

In the early grades, we had only one teacher for all grades. Fräulein Karsten, our third-grade teacher, stands out in my memory.

Her vacant stare and half-open mouth reminded me of one of our neighbor's chickens with a perennially open beak. She often criticized my penmanship for good reason. This teacher was very hard on some of the girls.

One in particular, Erika, had trouble catching on to basic arithmetic operations. In exasperation, Fräulein Karsten on more than one occasion pulled Erika by her blond curls out of the school bench, dragged her to the front of the class, and banged her head against the blackboard while shouting hysterically, "*Kein Pfund Lumpen bist Du wert* [You are not worth a pound of rags]!"

By chance, I met Erika again during one of my visits to Munich in 1964. I found her working in a beauty shop. She recognized me immediately, calling out, "*Schau, jetzt bin ich doch was geworden* [See, I did amount to something after all]."

Not all teachers were that fierce, but most were quick to deliver harsh reprimands. In hindsight, I wonder whether some were perhaps embittered war widows.

The only male on the faculty was a mild-mannered gentleman who taught religious studies. Later in the year, he introduced us to Joseph Ratzinger, future Cardinal and Pope Benedict XVI, now the late Pope Emeritus, whose short time with us I remember well.

A Special Teacher: "Even Pope—my teacher—Joseph Ratzinger always wrote back"[14]

My acquaintance with J.R. dates back to the early 1950s and our fourth-grade class in the Gebeleschule in Munich.

---

[14] First published in America: The Jesuit Review of Faith and Culture (June 11, 2018): 40-41.

Elementary schools at that time were still segregated according to gender before low enrollments brought boys and girls together a short time later. In our school, staffed by lady teachers, the only male we saw up close was the chaplain teaching our catechism class.

Herr Kaplan, as we called him, was short, stocky, and dark-haired with yellow-stained first and second fingers from cigarette smoking. His quiet, low-key demeanor seemed to complement his simple black suit and stiff white priest's collar. We thought he was alright.

One day, he informed our class that a new priest would be joining the diocese to prepare us for our First Communion, an important milestone in our lives, he said. We ten-year-olds were anxious and excited. What would he be like? Would he be nice to us? Would he like us? When the classroom door opened one morning, two black-clad gentlemen walked in: The first one we knew. The second one was young and slender, his suit too skimpy to fit his tall frame. He was our new teacher, introduced to us as Herr Ratzinger. He had just completed his seminary training in Freising, a town about twenty-five miles north of Munich.

From that day on, we fervently looked forward to our catechism class. We cheered the new man of the cloth as he entered our gray postwar school day. J.R.'s ecclesiastic knowledge seemed bottomless, his patience with us infinite. We duly intoned, *"Ecce Agnus Dei, Ecce qui tollis peccata mundi."* Of course, we translated all Latin phrases, but did we really understand what we were memorizing? I'm not sure any of us could have repeated his explanations of canonical law; but instead of scolding, he gently rephrased the questions to meet our way of reasoning. But what mattered most to us were his bright face and enthusiasm.

It was not to last. After only a short time, we learned that J.R. had suddenly and quietly left to pursue further studies at the university. We were inconsolable.

"We must write to him"! we said in a chorus. We debated endlessly. I can't recall the protocol we followed, but I was given the task of "secretary" to take down notes from class members and to transpose everyone's thoughts into words of disappointment and hope that he would return to us soon. I wrote the letter accordingly in the name of our class.

Did we really expect to hear from J.R.?

One day, I received a reply: A carefully drafted letter, an entire page, in his fine handwriting that almost resembled Arabic with its small, even, round letters, fluidly connected.

Forever the teacher, he wrote about the proper path to follow in growing up, illustrating it with an analogy: "If one buttons one's coat the wrong way, one would have to undo all of it and start over again to make it right," he wrote. "So it is with life," admonishing us, therefore, to choose the right beginning. And he signed it simply, "Joseph Ratzinger."

I no longer have that letter that I see so clearly in front of me. I must have lost it during my many moves. I continued my life with and without the Church, with and without family, with and without my homeland. And periodically, from a distance, I was able to follow his trajectory in the Church.

After more than thirty years, I decided to write to him, reminiscing about the early days in the Gebeleschule in

Munich. By then, he was in the Vatican as head of the Doctrine of the Faith. I did not expect to hear from him; but he graciously responded, sending me two small books he had written, *Feast of Faith* and *Liturgie und Kirchenmusik*, with a full-page, type-written, and signed letter.

In my letter to him, I had mentioned the fact that upon arriving in the United States and attending Sunday church services, I missed the music that had always accompanied such services at St. Michaels Kirche in Munich. I missed the Bach organ music, I missed the choir and full orchestra performing masses by Haydn and Mozart, music I had taken for granted growing up. I had simply lost my bond to the Church.

In his letter, he explained to me the deep connection between music and my belief. He encouraged me to seek that bridge in whatever music I have access to, to find that path again from music to liturgy.

I wrote to him once again at Christmas time. By then, he had become Pope Benedict XVI. He graciously sent his good wishes in a beautiful card depicting the Manger. He never left a note I sent unanswered.

This time, I will guard his writings.

The People: Portraits of the Students

We were all girls, about twenty-five in our class. When the boys joined us in fifth grade, they repaid our avid curiosity about them by aiming their slingshots with pellets at our calves after class. Beyond that, there was not much interaction between the two groups.

In the early fifties, a marked rise in economic status among some families was first noticeable in the better clothes that students began to wear. Class differences became obvious in carefully chosen attire, fastidious grooming, newfound self-confidence, and self-assurance. A new level of admiration made the rounds.

The economic gulf became a class divider. Groups formed sharing interests, leaving others out; the interaction between the favored and the less favored was minimal. I felt I did not belong anywhere, because even the less privileged seemed above me.

I was surprised, then, to become acquainted with a pretty girl, Evelyn, who lived with her family in a beautiful neighborhood villa. The building consisted of three floors, a vestibule filled with art objects and a salon furnished with exquisite furniture.

How could it be that after living through a war, this family resided in an undamaged grand house on an estate-size property? Had they not been in the same war as the rest of us? What were they doing during the war? To this day, I cannot answer my question.

But I soon found the answer to Evelyn's interest in me. Her parents had asked her to choose me for help with basic arithmetic problems, gratuitously of course, in exchange for the privilege of being near her and being invited into her house. Our friendship did not last.

Christine Kaufmann: Not Just Another Student
Christine joined our school for a few weeks in the 1950s.

She was a child actress. After leaving us, she acted in movies and later married the American actor Tony Curtis.

You couldn't get near her, because she was always surrounded by a group of eager girls interested in her and in her early career. She was certainly lovely, but she was not the only one.

Christine stood out by her controlled comportment and her carefully orchestrated grooming. Her clothes must have been custom-made, because nothing like them was available even in the most expensive stores. Rows of ruffles and ribbons were stitched in different angles into the unusual fabric. A huge satin ribbon of various colors was artfully wound into her shiny honey-brown hair. She was pleasant but knew how to keep us at arm's length.

Christine was not with us for long. She was whisked away for some acting assignment, leaving us with images of a glamorous interlude in our drab postwar school days.

Years later, I saw an iconic Hollywood photo of her with Tony Curtis and Cary Grant. After her divorce from Tony Curtis, she returned to Munich, where she died of leukemia in 2017.

Social Class Differences: Steps to Higher Education

Economic differences became evident in the classroom, in the teachers, and in the students. They even reached beyond school walls, with a profound effect on the next level of education. In the tiered system of German education, children took the education department examinations to enter the *Gymnasium*[15] after the fourth or fifth grade, allowing two tries. Who made the decision about who was allowed to sit for the tests? Parents and teachers.

Not one word about the process of applying for entry to the *Gymnasium* was mentioned in our class. One day, certain students were absent, because they were taking the requisite examinations for the next step. A month or so later, the teacher announced those students' success on the tests. We were surprised to hear that a girl with D grades passed. Her parents had hired private tutors to help her, we learned. A classmate and I held the best class grade record, but we were ignorant of the test procedure and protocol, an opportunity that was supposed to be open to all. How could that happen?

Our teachers were well aware of the economic standing of their students and their parents. It was considered unrealistic of students from underprivileged backgrounds to aim for the *Gymnasium*, the path leading to university, even if their grades warranted it. Such parents could not possibly afford to keep their children attending school for years when they should be learning a trade after the eighth grade and going to work. It was not even a topic for discussion. One had to depend on one's teacher, then, to become aware of this opportunity. It would not even have occurred to us to ask; how could we ask for something we didn't know existed?

After students spent nine successful years and passed their final examinations in the *Gymnasium*, they were granted the

---

[15] The Gymnasium, a derivative of the ancient Greek sports arena, is comparable to a preparatory high school in the United States, comparable to the French Lycée.

Abitur certification, a permanent class distinction that separated them from those who did not have it, like Dr. Seuss's "Sneetches" without the chicken-on-the-chest mark.

Today, many students in Germany reach that level of higher education; too many, some say. However, according to current news reports, children from working-class families still have hurdles to overcome.

What School Vacations Were Like

Short trips and vacation destinations, too, were good indicators of class differences. Over the weekend or for longer stays during semester breaks, parents took their children in the family car over the Brenner Pass to Lake Garda or Lake Como in Italy. The Brenner Pass in the Alps was, and still is, considered the gateway to happiness, because in two hours one crossed from gray Germany into sunny Italy. Others took the train to visit the Alps, staying in local bed-and-breakfasts. Among those who could afford to travel, even the type of luggage and matching clothes were economic indicators. The rest of us, whose parents could not afford such excursions, stayed home to help in the household or to be with like friends.

Did we ever have fun at our school? Was the regimentation ever interrupted for festive occasions, for holidays? I recall two events: Christmas and Mardi Gras.

Christmas 1950

Our third-grade teacher asked us to bring a small bough from a fir tree decorated for the season.

I hated to come home with school requests, because they usually involved money, but this one should be fairly simple, even during those lean postwar years.

Vati cut a nice branch off the spruce in our yard. *But how should I decorate it?* I wondered. Tante Meta, my foster aunt, grappled with my assignment and came up with the idea of a star made of straw.

From the shed, she brought a few pieces of straw, laid them out on the kitchen table, cut them, flattened them, bound them into a multi-rayed star, and tied it to the branch, a piece of *Handarbeit* [hand-made craft]. At least I had something to take to class for the Christmas celebration.

With that offering in hand, I walked to school.

I opened the door to a warm, festive classroom. What beautiful boughs everyone had trimmed with tinsel, cinnamon star cookies, *Lebkuchen* [gingerbread] Santa Clauses, butter cookies shaped like Christmas ornaments decorated with colorful frosting and sprinkles.

Fräulein Karsten, our teacher, decided that we should exchange boughs with each other. A flurry of activity ensued, with little girls running around, carrying their laden branches to the new owners. Most of them knew with whom they wanted to trade.

I had been alright until then. I knew better than to expect someone to trade with me—cookies for a piece of straw?

After the excitement settled, Fräulein Karsten noticed that Annie and I still had not traded with anyone. Standing next to me, Annie held her plain fir branch with only a bar of soap tied on top. The soap came wrapped in shiny olive-green foil-like paper with large black lettering, spelling "Palmolive." Had her parents been in a quandary, as mine had been, about how to decorate something with nothing? In desperation, had they sent her off with that piece of soap?

But in those early postwar years, a bar of soap <u>was</u> something, especially "Palmolive." It was American. It smelled nice. It could be used for many ablutions. It was hard to get. It cost who-knows-how-much.

I knew better than to expect Annie to trade with me. But we did as we were told, trading a straw star for a piece of soap, called "Palmolive."

Mardi Gras 1952

Fräulein Zehetmaier, our fifth-grade teacher, asked us to appear in costume on Fat Tuesday. We could not guess, from her orders and the usual prevailing atmosphere of strict discipline, that it was supposed to be a fun affair.

In the depth of winter, I hoped for a costume simulating a peach blossom. To accommodate my wishes, my foster aunt started sewing together pieces of cloth by hand, using some yards of pink tulle hidden in the garret. Stringing together tiny colored glass beads, one at a time, she wound them, ribbon-like, into my hair.

Tante Meta kept stitching and was still sewing on that Tuesday morning when it was time for me to leave. I kept pressing her. I was going to be late, which meant having to stay after school to make up for lost time, the usual punishment. Finally, the last stitch sewed, knot tied, thread cut. I was off.

I remember the shoes with flat thin soles I was wearing on my hurried walk to school. There were no snowplows where we lived and certainly no school buses. I started walking, slipping with every step in shoes that had no traction. I felt as though I were trying to do somersaults. A couple of cars passed me on that lonely road. One driver was grinning at the clownish figure I must have cut as I was trying to keep my balance, arms flailing.

I was late, of course, so I slithered into the school building, joining a happy class with schoolmates wearing outrageous makeup and colorful outfits, with confetti flying everywhere.

Then Erna, another student, sauntered into the classroom. She was even later than I was. She wore her usual plain woolen school dress to which she had added a single Mardi Gras concession: A large blood-red crepe paper poppy pinned behind her ear. That was it.

The teacher did not even notice that Erna was late, nor that she was not wearing a costume. But the boys noticed her, she with a slight gap between her square front teeth, and that red poppy glowing against her high cheekbone. They started whispering, grinning, looking slyly at her, elbowing each other. My frilly dress and beads, labors that had pushed my foster aunt to the limit, went unnoticed. I didn't get it. I did much later. It's called "sex appeal."

The Album

During a visit to Munich in 1990, Adi, my foster brother, handed me an album he had saved for me, dating back to my school days in the early 50s. It was customary then to pass around the booklet, asking teachers and schoolmates, and even parents, to write a poem or a saying as a remembrance. I am sure that I, too, had been asked to contribute. What did I write? I don't recall.

My own album shows twelve students' verses: Carefully written words on the right side of each page, accompanied by a drawing or a colorful sticker representing flowers on the left side. Each signed entry bears a date; for example, October 15, 1953, February 21, 1954.

What touched me after so many years were the laudable penmanship, artistic expression, and pensive words.

Perhaps I had not given credit previously to the forbearance of our elementary school teachers or to the curriculum. The exacting penmanship I could trace to our class instruction, but who taught us such dignified verses? What were their sources? Here are two examples:

Trübt sich Dein Lebenslauf
Blicke zum Vater auf
Menschen lass Menschen sein
Helfen kann Gott allein.

Im Glauben klar
In Liebe wahr
In Hoffnung fröhlich immerdar.

Author's translation:
If your life does not go well
Look up to the Father

Let people be people
Only God can help.

Clear in belief
True in love
Happy in hope always.

Were we really that mature as eleven- and twelve-year-olds? Whatever the interpretation, one thing was definitely lacking in the album entries: Humor. No jokes, no funny sayings. We were earnest.

Chapter V: Nature, My Redemption

Nature, my steady companion, was ever present in our yard, the neighbors' yards, the meadow across from us, and the park, the English Garden, across the street.

The Gardens

I felt closest to nature in the summer, when I climbed the brittle ladder with a couple of steps missing, leading to the flat veranda roof. With my back against the last of the wall, I sat up there alone watching the sun slowly inch up on the horizon, lighting every dew drop, making the damp flora below shimmer and glisten. The entire panorama was spread before and around me. I could barely detect audible sounds and tiny movements as grasses and flowers bent by the weight of the night's moisture tried to lift themselves up slowly. A lark called.

Among our garden verdure was an unlikely ornamental species, a cultivated double-blossom almond tree. Who had planted it? How long ago? It was already there to greet us when we came to Tivoli. It had been heavily pruned so that its thin, long switches grew densely out of the rounded trunk top, making it look like Struwwelpeter, the German children's book character with long hair sticking straight out from his scalp. In spring, pale pink blossoms imitating buttons of silk rosettes dotted the length of each branch in tight rows, forming an arching bough. I feared for the fragile blossoms when a fierce spring wind battered them and tore off barely sprouted leaves. No visitor to Tivoli wanted to leave without carrying home an example that my foster father had cut off, however reluctantly.

The neglected neighbor gardens had their own wild charm with their overgrown thickets: Mounds of nettles I learned to avoid, letting the insects nibble at their syrupy blossoms; hazelnut trees I learned to climb to harvest their ripening nuts.

The Meadow

Outside our garden gate was the Tivoli meadow undisturbed by human traffic except for my scampering, or so I thought. Once or twice I did come across strange white, opaque pieces of rubber resembling large thumbs that left me wondering. Who had left them lying in the grass? What purpose did they serve? The answer would have to wait a few years.

But then, it was summer, and the meadow outside our garden fence was thick with wildflowers and tall grasses that reached to my thighs. My preferred place to lie was on the ground among the green stems and blades, looking up into the sky, and watching the white, cottony clouds glide by. I imagined their forms representing fairy tale figures or animals for which I invented names.

Another world was coming alive down below. Tiny critters of various sizes, shapes, and colors scurried along the dry dirt, climbed up halfway on a grass stem, and unable to hold on any longer, dropped to the ground. Or they flew onto a neighboring wildflower, a bluebell, a poppy, a cornflower. Or they chased each other off, one tiny speck of a bug pursuing another. They were busy chewing on a leaf, copulating in twos or threes, holding still. It was a universe in miniature, each creature seeking its own space and fulfilling its mission of existing.

The English Garden

And across the street was the English Garden. It was, and still is, a 1.4-square-mile park, larger than New York City's Central Park, created in 1789 for the Prince of Bavaria by Sir Benjamin Thompson, later Count Rumford. The park was laid out in the English style, giving nature priority over the manicuring shears of the French model.

At the edge of the park, untamed bushes of hawthorn, acorn, and elm saplings bent high over the bicycle path next to the street. The dense foliage of sated green was interspersed here and there with the dark red of the blood-beeches, all of it barely permitting a view of the park's interior.

Inside the park, raked walking paths separated clearings of untamed lawns amid the canopy of deciduous trees of all manner and a few conifers. Periodically, the forest department crew trimmed the grassy areas and removed dead wood and brush from beneath the spirea bushes and trees.

I used to roam in the park for hours. In the groves, I loved to hear the wind soughing through the treetops. On still days, I could hear the tiny critters whispering.

Among the abundance of vegetation, I always discovered new weeds and grasses, or a hidden flower. On one occasion, I found some mushrooms. I brought them home. Tante Meta called them *Morcheln* [Morels]. She sent me for more, admonishing me to be careful not to disturb the tiny root bulge submerged below the dirt. She cooked them to everyone's delight. Now I see these Morels on expensive restaurant menus.

I have even tasted wild wood strawberries. I shall never forget them. I found them during my wanderings there. They are not only hard to find but hard to see, because they hide below in the shadowy thicket. The ripe berry is a tiny, dark wine-red, thimble-shaped cone that could not even fit over the tip of my little finger. Their perfume is intense, aromatic, and ambrosial. I kept returning each season to the spot where I had found them originally, but luck had been with me only once. Perhaps I could have been mistaken about the original place, but I knew that part of the park like I knew my backyard.

The first sign of fall was usually the appearance of the purple single-blossom autumn crocus, followed soon by dropped pods releasing their seeds from chestnut trees. It would not be long before I could gather the dark-brown shiny nuts and roast them until the skin split, revealing the edible yellowish, mealy interior. Do they still roast chestnuts in little stands on the streets in town, or are there just too many options today for myriad snacks and diversions?

During the winter months, the English Garden seemed forsaken by visitors. Frost disguised spindly gray tree branches. The cold sheathed the willow branches in clear ice, making them sing as the wind played with them. Snow packed its soft blanket over the bare flora like a protective hood during the winter sleep, preserving the sap for spring rebirth. If one walked softly and was not afraid of getting lost in the white landscape, one could sometimes hear a sudden faint dribble of powdery snow dusting down from above, turning into a mini-avalanche when a snowpack loosened from a big branch. Too much snow could make it snap under the weight when it turned heavy and wet.

When my foster father brought home my first skates (a pair he found at a scrap metal dealer), I tried them out on the Kleinhesseloher See, a small man-made lake, in the park. They were the screw-on variety that had a tendency to come loose from my shoes. Even so, it was magical on a wintry Sunday morning to skate in a hidden cove on the lake, with no one else around. The surface was not smooth. There were frosted ripples and bumps, and patches of snow-covered areas of clear, thinly frozen greenish ice. I soon learned to retreat when I heard the first crackling in the ice. But I was entranced by the stillness of the white, icy scene.

When snow turned to slush in mud season, and a myriad of rivulets sprang forth, I could detect the brown sheaths covering the tight leaf buds emerging on trees and bushes. With warmer rays of sun, they would break open to reveal leaves, at first yellowish, then turning into a translucent spring green. Green gasses poked through the furrows and clods of dirt that had begun to dry out.

Pussy willows were always early messengers of spring by the Kleinhesseloher See in the park. Two white-blooming flowers began appearing in succession in early March: First came the pure-white snowdrops, followed later by the slightly bigger snowflakes, distinguished by a tiny green dot on each white blossom leaf. Soon came wild crocuses and the yellow cowslips. Seemingly overnight, a carpet of feathery green with white star-like flowers, the wood anemones, covered the ground among dark tree trunks. The anemones were evenly spaced as if measured out by a superior maker, a picture not unlike a Gobelin tapestry.

Blossoms came before leaves on some of the bushes and trees. The forsythia on the corner of the entrance to the English Garden made me stop to take in the show. From a tangle of naked beige and gray sticks in winter, tiny paper-thin brown husks started to peek out that slowly released still-folded blossoms of yellow four-petal flowers. They crowded each stem from the base to the top, forming a golden rod. Soon, the branches revealed a hint of green leaves to come.

In one's wandering, one might come upon a wild plum sowing its jewel-like white blossoms among the dark branches of the surrounding trees. Once, a group of people assembled in the park near a thicket. It was unusual to see such a crowd, because nothing else around showed any signs of spring. Clustered near a wild plum, the murmuring crowd was enchanted by the veil of delicate blossoms, as if the tree were weeping in bloom. Would people become that excited today about seeing a common plum?

Other varieties showed flowers only after their leaves had sprouted. The red- or white-blooming hawthorns and the candle-like blossom stalks of the horse chestnuts waited until May, along with the narcotically sweet scent of the linden tree clusters. By then, surrounded by that abundance, a visitor would not even notice the tiny blossoms of the oaks.

Hidden among the foliage in the English Garden was a small wooden shack by the Kleinhesseloher See. During the hot summer days, my foster parents occasionally sent me there for ice cream. I held up my little pot, and the lady on duty would drop in a few scoops. I ran home as fast as I could to prevent them from melting completely.

The shack has become the Seehaus, a busy restaurant with outdoor tables, benches, and chairs—you're lucky if you can garner a free spot today. Flocks of ducks cruise on the lake but were once used for target practice by American soldiers during the Allied occupation of Munich, according to my foster brother Adi.

Scattered among the park trees were man-made structures that fed my childhood fantasy about past sojourners. For example, the Rumford Haus, built in the Palladian style in 1791, used to be an officers' mess. It stood vacant for a long time. Whose ghosts lived there before it was finally converted to a children's center? Or on a hill, I climbed the Monopteros, an Apollo temple built in 1832 in the Greek style with Ionic columns. Today, it is a favorite resting place and lookout point made for selfies.

And I often visited the five-story *Chinesische Turm* [Chinese Tower], a pagoda built of wood, the original structure dating to 1789. Today, it serves as a restaurant and bandstand. It has become a favorite of members of the annual Kocherl Ball (cooks' or servants' ball), the largest outdoor dance festival in Munich dating back to 1900. Participants dressed in the traditional Bavarian costumes arrive as early as six in the morning to secure a space. They dance to a live orchestra. Hours later, they leave the surrounding grassy areas trampled into muddy clumps for the forest department workers to rehabilitate.

In my youth, the park revealed some structures that may have gone unnoticed by other visitors, like secrets here and there, hidden low under the green shadows. I found a weathered moss-covered stone bench, or even an exedra, semicircular in shape, with a curved back and armrest. Who had lingered there? Who had built it, when, and for whom?

The beautiful English Garden has become much used, sometimes abused, by huge crowds visiting during the pleasant seasons.

The English Garden, the meadow, our garden, and those of the neighbors all were my home. They were not only part of my life, they were my life. They relieved my loneliness. I never questioned their existence, their purpose, or their relevance, though I questioned so much else. I had a simple but intense attachment to nature.

Chapter VI: The End of Tivoli

B y living at the edge of town, we were not only geographically separated from the rest of Munich, we were basically removed from everything going on in society. With no telephone, no radio, no newspapers that we could afford, we were isolated.

Around 1954, a city utility workman planted a tall wooden pole outside our fence and strung electric wire to connect it to our roof. And there was light in our hut. No more kerosene lamps and candles. We never did have running water. The hand pump in the yard persisted, as did the outhouse in the corner.

With electricity installed, Adi was now able to connect his new Grundig-brand radio. A new world opened for me. Alone at home, I fiddled with the knobs and came upon music such as I had never heard before. It was so beautiful, I started to cry. When Vati came home and saw me thus entranced, he forbade me to ever listen to that *Zeug* [stuff] again. "*Das macht melancholisch* [It will make you melancholy]," he said. But I was sold. I could carry a tune well and loved melodies.

By then, I was saying my first goodbye to Tivoli. I was

moving to the St. Anna Heim. Seven years later, emigrating to the United States, I bid my *adieu*.

Returning to Germany for a visit in 1964, I found our Tivoli hut sealed off and taped with municipal placards proclaiming the building unsafe for entry. It was destined for a quick tear-down and removal. Vati had been dead for three years, and Adi had left for an apartment closer to town. Herbert, the oldest son, was the last inhabitant. He was evicted and placed in a care home for men.

Today, a large hotel occupies the Tivoli property. The mill still stands.

What is left of Tivoli? Only memories. Is the ornamental almond tree still standing, holding the souls of my late foster parents in its spring bloom?

PART II: THE CATHOLIC SISTERS OF THE ST. ANNA HEIM (1954-1961)

Why would any mother send her daughter to live in a home for children directed by *Schwestern* [Catholic Sisters]? It was not because she did not love her child or neglect her. On the contrary, this was 1954, a time when it was still considered *de rigueur* to send the daughter of a good family to spend a year in a private home guided by nuns, who belonged to a convent that provided room and board. Such a stay represented part of a girl's formation. Only parents of a certain social stratum could afford that.

My case was different. I was there at the courtesy of the city or the state.

The Sisters of the St. Anna Heim consisted of a group of young and not-so-young women who had taken the veil following a religious order, called Niederbronner, to dedicate their lives to serving others. They had chosen to shepherd a flock of growing girls into adulthood, patiently putting up with the caprices of adolescents who outnumbered them about five to one. Adi remarked more than once that he would rather take care of a sack of fleas than supervise that swarm of juveniles.

The Sisters performed all chores of cooking and cleaning. It was a big change for me, coming from a home in Tivoli where I had to help in the house and yard from an early age on. I had moved from a poor to a privileged situation.

The Place: Impressions of St. Anna Heim

The three-story gray-stucco building of the Heim stood on the corner of Prinzregentenstrasse and Oettingenstrasse. Across the street at right angles was a huge block-long building, the American Allied PX (post exchange) and former headquarters of the German Luftwaffe.

An iron gate with a buzzer closed off the Heim from the sidewalk. The gate opened to a small concrete area with steps leading to the main door of the building, which in turn led to a tiny reception cubicle where one of the Sisters, our Cerberus, kept track of the traffic, more of it incoming than outgoing. The Sisters were responsible for our security, protecting us from unwanted visitors.

Who were our visitors? Parents of the girls, delivery people, and members of other religious orders. And beggars. In the case of beggars, the Sister on duty emerged from her cage, reached sideways under her ample gray apron, and extracted a piece of bread.

She handed it benevolently to the petitioner, a man in tatters, or a war-injured invalid. He responded with a halfgenuflecting pose, murmuring a blessed *Dankeschön*.

I, too, was once a petitioner of sorts. After my foster mother died, Tante Meta took care of our household. But after a year, she had had enough of our hard, shabby way of living in a hut without even the most basic amenities. Besides, she was homesick for her hometown in the east where she had grown up and lived surrounded by family. Before she left Munich, she tried to place me with the Sisters.

Such space at the St. Anna Heim was limited to one or two openings for city-sponsored girls who were parentless. Tante Meta kept prodding me to stop by repeatedly after school to check my status on the waiting list. I was an eleven-year-old girl asking about a room at the inn. The nuns accepted me in 1954.

A new world opened to me when I arrived: Living together in the same quarters with a large group of about forty girls ages twelve to eighteen meant a lesson in democracy in that all of us had to obey the same rules and follow the same routine. We shared the food and the rooms, even though we had come from greatly different backgrounds.

Chapter I: My First Night at the Sisters

We slept seventeen to a room—not quite like in a Ludwig Bemelmans'[16] illustration of a group of little girls lined up piously in identical beds, but close. A Sister came to bid us good night, switching off the light at nine p.m., admonishing us to cease all conversation. My neighbor, Ursula, was curious about me. She asked me about myself and my family. I was torn between wanting to obey the house rules and trying to answer the questions of my new acquaintance. I was eager to make new friends, so I replied in short answers.

Suddenly, the light switched on, and the supervising Sister appeared. "Who spoke?" she asked.

I hesitantly raised my hand. I was mortified. My new friend did not come to my aid. My first night there, and I was already marked as a miscreant. The Sister called me outside. "Why did you not obey the curfew?" she questioned. I tried to explain, feeling like a criminal. I was sent back to bed to

---

[16] Ludwig Bemelmans, Austrian-American writer and illustrator of children's books (1898-1962).

repent. What an inauspicious beginning. A first lesson learned, having to choose between trying to make friends and obeying the rules. Each had its price.

I fell asleep to the strident tinkle of the streetcar bell and awoke to it as well, because the tram stop was right outside our building. The cars and delivery vans made their familiar stopping and starting noises, beginning with the early traffic around five in the morning and not subsiding until past our bedtime.

Chapter II: The People: Portraits of the Sisters

What we saw of the Sisters was their ankle-length black habit hiding all but their hands and faces from the chin to the eyebrow. A black veil covered a white cap, coif, and guimpe shielding the rest of their facial features and throat. A large wooden crucifix hung suspended from a cord around the neck down to the middle of the chest. Every nun had a rosary of wooden beads attached to the waistband with a metal crucifix dangling at the end that reached below the knee.

Sister Arilde was overseeing us daily and checking on us periodically at night. She was tall and slender. Under her coif, the visible part of her pretty pale face was crowned by quasi-Frida Kahlo[17] eyebrows that tended to knit even closer together when we misbehaved.

On more serious occasions, her lips turned into a wriggly line like that of a discombobulated Charlie Brown in the Peanuts comic strip. She spent the most time with us, so we learned to read her moods and behave accordingly. Sister

---

[17] Frida Kahlo (1907-1954), Mexican artist.

Arilde was fair. We respected her.

Sister Adelaria was the organist who came alive when she played and sang hymns. She prodded our tone-deaf choristers to try their utmost at practice sessions. We were not taught to read music. We simply guessed at the up-and-down path of the black dots on the choir book page.

I was asked to join a group of three other girls to sing in a quartet. One girl, tiny, freckle-faced, toothy Louise, could harmonize better than any of us. In her company, I was embarrassed to sing my middle part. I preferred singing in the choir, because I was able to blend in with the entire group. But in the quartet, each of us had a melody line to harmonize with the other three. It became painfully obvious when I missed a note, as I often did.

Sister Aurelia, whom we glimpsed here and there, moved in mincing steps as if she were a slowly moving vat. She was exceedingly heavy, her sweaty, rosy cheeks bulging beneath her white coif. She was the cook and probably the bottle-washer, too, with a work apron twisted around her at all times. Of all the Sisters, she was the sweetest. Whenever she could, she sneaked us a slice of freshly baked bread, her pudgy hands indicating conspiratorial silence.

Frau Oberin was the head mistress of the St. Anna Heim. A hush fell over us whenever we heard the staccato clip of her heels in the corridor. Her bird-of-prey gray eyes seized us briefly before she vanished into another room. With ramrod-straight posture, she folded her lower arms and hands beneath the bib of her apron, making her chest appear like that of a duck.

Just by chance, I saw her once near tears. Holding a letter, she stood in a corner of the hallway with two other Sisters. Judging from the few words I overheard, I sensed that she had just received orders to move to a similar home in another city. The deep emotion she expressed betrayed her reluctance to leave. The other Sisters tried to comfort her in hushed tones. Nuns, like priests, take the vows of obedience. Orders were orders. She had to leave.

Most of the other Sisters worked behind the scenes, so we seldom saw them. Like a shadow, one would occasionally flit past, disappearing into their communal quarters. We did not observe them interacting in a personal way other than in customary greetings. They limited their public communication to issues concerning us. Their cloistered world was off limits to us.

The Sisters seldom left the St. Anna Heim. But the month of May presented an occasion. They led us to a neighborhood church for the weekly *Maiandacht* [May church service] dedicated to the Mother of God. It was an evening service, and I looked forward to walking near the Isar river, watching the streetlamps' mellow yellow light penetrate the nascent spring-green leaves of the elm trees that lined the sidewalk. The nature scene and the church music made the outing pleasant for me.

We knew very little about the time the nuns spent away from us. What other activities did they pursue? We learned that they performed charitable work beyond taking care of us. In one instance, a small group of us was asked at Christmas to sing at the bedside of a dying lady. I was impressed by the profound gentleness with which the Sisters treated the sick.

We often guessed about the lives of the Sisters. We tried to fathom what went on behind closed doors. Why did they choose such a life? What had they escaped from? Would they return to the real world if they could?

Did the Sisters ever ask any of us whether we wanted to join their order? Sister Arilde did ask me once in a mild voice, suggesting that I would be taken care of for life, that I would not have many cares. I would never have to worry about a drunken husband coming home. I was familiar with men's drunkenness from Vati's periodic episodes in Tivoli, but in those days we always got over them in the end. I knew too little about the nuns' secretive lives to be tempted by her offer. I can't recall my answer. I probably looked stunned at her question. *Did she ask other girls?* I wondered.

An incident I later observed from a distance gave me pause. In the hallway, Sister Arilde, agitated but controlled as only nuns can be, leaned into a very young woman who was wearing the customary white Cistercian habit of another order. I couldn't very well eavesdrop. The next day, I saw that very lady in civilian clothes. I recognized her facial features immediately. I assumed she had decided to leave the order. The 1959 film *The Nun's Story* recaptured that scene for me. By the end of that movie, the character played by Audrey Hepburn had exchanged her nun's habit for simple civilian attire, leaving the confines of the cloister for good.

Chapter III: Group Portrait of the Girls

After having been without close friends in Tivoli in my early youth, I was now suddenly surrounded by many girls of my age. They formed a happy, pleasant group who allowed me to transition quickly to my new life. I got along well with groups, but I was never able to form individual bonds, with one exception: Gertraud, who became a lifelong friend. Gertraud and her parents accepted me despite our social differences.

Our friendship extended beyond the walls of the Heim. I recall a special weekend outing with Gertraud's parents to one of the ponds near Munich. They invited me for lunch in a lakeside restaurant. I believe we ate baked trout with potato salad and vegetables.

Would I be able to handle a trout with head, tail, and skin intact? I did. After all, I remembered seeing Vati on many occasions filleting raw herring before marinating it. Riding in their car on the way home in the dark, I was fascinated by the string of white headlights coming toward us from one direction and the row of red rear fender lights we followed in the opposite direction. It was my first car ride.

Like Gertraud, most of the girls came from families who still maintained their villas, their cars, their comfortable lifestyles. Many of them lived out of town, some in villages in the Bavarian Alps. The parents, well-dressed and self-assured, often checked on their daughters at the Sisters.

My foster family, with the exception of my foster brother, Adi, seldom visited me. When they did come, they stood out in their threadbare clothes and in their diffident comportment. They used public transportation, while the other parents drove up in their expensive sedans. Occasionally, the parents who could afford it slipped the Sisters a pound of fresh coffee beans, perhaps the only real coffee the Sisters ever had.

The same contrast in type of clothing and degree of self-assurance held true for the daughters of these well-established families. I could not compete, nor did I try. Long ago, in Kindergarten, I had learned that some people were better off than others. I just accepted it. It must be said, though, that the girls wore and displayed their wealth lightly. I can't recall instances of overt bragging or flaunting, nor did I feel any discrimination.

School choice was another divider that separated us. The Heim provided room and board, as well as study facilities. Formal education took place mostly at a private Catholic school off campus. One or two welfare residents like me went instead to the nearest public school, because the city did not cover private education. If there were qualitative differences between these two school systems, I was not aware of them.

I was too busy keeping up with my assignments.

Weekend plans, too, exposed class distinctions. Every other weekend, as was the rule, most of the girls were whisked away in the family car for either a trip home or a short vacation in northern Italy. Instead of taking time off, those who had no other place to go stayed with the Sisters and were sometimes corralled into helping them peel potatoes or prepare other vegetables for dinner.

Future plans also made a difference among us. Many of the girls' plans followed their parents' wishes to continue their studies at the university or work in their parents' businesses. Some had no career ambitions at the moment; they just wanted to spend some time at their families' homes before deciding which path to take.

My thoughts circled around the idea of pursuing music studies, but I did not know how to proceed. I didn't even try to ask the Sisters or schoolteachers, because a music career seemed rather unrealistic. I wanted to become an opera or *Lieder* singer. When I asked Vati for his opinion, he warned me that such a career path often leads through the beds of directors. That answered my question.

But the Sisters came to my aid in another way, suggesting a more practical goal. They said that my grades qualified me to take the entrance examination to enter *Mittelschule* [middle school], preparing me for a white-collar job. I followed their advice.

Counterbalance to Social Differences

At the Sisters, differences among us were mitigated by our

prevailing need to follow the same rules: Exhibit unconditional respect toward the Sisters and toward each other. Maintain appropriate personal hygiene and neatness in appearance. Appear on time for meals. Prepare school assignments conscientiously. Participate in Catholic mass twice weekly. Sing in the choir whether or not we could carry a tune.

Temporary jealousies occasionally developed among small cliques of friends, but any differences were quickly resolved. The democratic atmosphere and the prevailing spirit of camaraderie eliminated overt prejudices. We all lived there. We all got along—a great lesson learned.

Chapter IV: Rooms Bearing Witness - The Washroom

ornings followed a routine. Three adjacent bedrooms were on the second floor. Sister Arilde woke us by entering briskly, clapping her hands sharply.

We charged out of our beds and headed for the washroom. Against the wall, about a dozen sinks lined up in a row with mirrors above them. We were given limited time to brush our teeth and finish our ablutions by washing ourselves to the waist with a washrag. The rag was the typical European kind, sewn shut on three sides, like a mitt.

We were bashful. We wore pajamas, so we took off only our jacket, leaving on the under-shirt and long pants. We made an art out of washing ourselves beneath that shirt without exposing our budding breasts. Furtively, we glanced around to see whether we could spy tiny protuberances to compare with our own. A quick hair comb, a garment slipped on, and we were ready for the day.

No, not for breakfast, but for mass twice a week. We trooped into the small private chapel, where Sister Adelaria was already playing the harmonium. No priest was present. We simply knelt, prayed, and sang hymns. The service lasted only about half an hour. I had trouble kneeling for so long on bare-wood benches. Sometimes I fainted, probably because of my empty stomach. The Sisters helped me up and onto the seat of the bench, but as soon as I came to, it was back to kneeling again. During certain times of the year, like *Fasching* [Mardi Gras] and the Oktoberfest, we were asked to pray for the sins of the world. We were clueless about those sins. Later, it dawned on us that those holidays were considered wild times, during which people partied, drank, and committed sins.

Once a month, we were allowed to take a bath in the cellar that contained a couple of tubs. Additional baths cost fifty cents in today's currency, but only those with pocket money took advantage of that offer.

How, then, did we keep clean? In the corner of our washroom was a makeshift "shower" :

A sink and a plastic curtain on a metal rod. It was the only place where one could stand in the nude and wash down. Once during my procedure, Sister Arilde suddenly pulled back the curtain and just stood there looking at me. *What was she thinking?* I wondered, seeing a skinny thirteen-year-old with a flat chest. Without a word, she pulled the curtain shut again and left. I continued my bath.

The Dining Hall

After our pious start in the chapel, we rushed to the dining hall for breakfast, where tables arranged end to end with chairs on both sides awaited us. We spooned thin marmalade onto a slice of *Mischbrot* (a mixture of light and dark bread that was chewy and faintly yeasty-tasting). We tried our best to keep the jam from running through the holes of the thin slice and onto our fingers and hands. No butter. We drank a type of nutty coffee with milk. And then off to school.

Lunch was an irregular affair as we returned from our schools at different hours. But at dinner, we were all together, always curious about the menu. Sometimes, only pancakes were served. Meat came in small portions and consisted of the beef-stew variety. One time, a couple of slices of salami were so thin they seemed transparent. But these were still the early 1950s, and the Sisters were trying to make ends meet.

Helping to supplement my diet on occasion was Adi, who appeared at the gate with a bag containing a loaf of fresh bread, a stick of butter, and a jar of jam, all of which I devoured in no time.

The Study Halls

They consisted of three adjacent rooms connected by doors. We studied hard. There wasn't much else to occupy our time, because extra-curricular activities as we know them did not exist, neither at the Sisters nor at school—not even sports. We recognized the importance of good grades for our standing in class and at the Sisters. We did not question the relevance of assignments and tests.

Most of the girls studied in groups, because they attended the private Catholic school administered by another group of nuns off campus. I was the only one in my grade to attend public school. I was therefore on my own with my schoolwork.

Exit examinations to qualify for diplomas, be they for the *Abitur* [top level] or the *Mittlere Reife* [middle level], were prescribed by Munich's department of education. We found them difficult and prepared accordingly by using old sample booklets with listed questions and answers. After completing our daily school assignments, we delved into these booklets, working on the problems for hours. It was not unusual to spend an entire school year preparing for this goal.

Study curfew was at nine p.m., but we used flashlights to study beneath our bed covers, not letting light peek through the tucked-in edges. It didn't work. In a pitch-dark sleeping hall, a thin yellow ray always managed to escape. Punishment in this case was usually a mild reprimand to get back to rest. Intrepid young scholars would lock themselves into toilet stalls to study. The tall walls and the doors of the stalls were built to reach from floor to ceiling. There were no gaps below like those in the United States. But light is like water—it finds its own level, and the Sisters knew that. It was impossible for us to hide.

Elective Studying

A shiny Steinway grand piano stood off to the side in the largest study hall. It was locked, except for practice time. Who was allowed to practice? Only those who had private lessons offered off campus. For them, one of the Sisters unlocked the piano lid and uncovered the keys protected by a red velvet strip with golden tassels at both ends—a deferential moment for me, watching as a bystander. I admired the student pianists. I wished to be one of them but did not have the means. What a wonder to be able to wring out a melody from the black behemoth with the ivory teeth. Singing seemed so simple by comparison. And it's free. One always has the instrument at the ready. One is the instrument.

"Extra-curricular Activities"

A black-and-white television set stood in one of the study halls. Every so often, the Sisters tuned in to the German version of *Father Knows Best.* We eagerly lined up our chairs as if we were indeed going to the movies. The Sisters were in charge of the control knob. One of them stood silently next to the TV for the duration of the program. This particular show of comfortable American family life seemed unreal to me in the 1950s, because it was so far removed from my surroundings. For the Sister, though, this version was all too realistic at times. When she deemed certain scenes inappropriate to our age group, she repeatedly interrupted the broadcast. For example, when Jim Anderson, playing the father, so much as hinted at affection toward Margaret, his TV wife, the Sister used the controls to cause immediate *Bildstörung* [picture distortion], showing crazy black-and-white waves and wriggles zigzagging across the screen. We viewers did allow ourselves some covert snickering or eye-rolling before returning to our schoolwork, our own reality.

I can't recall other occasions of television viewing. We did not see the TV news, for instance, no movies, nor was there a radio available. Our lives were truly confined within the walls of the St. Anna Heim and controlled by the nuns.

How did we spend our free time? We chatted about parents and relatives; we fantasized about weekend and vacation plans; we gabbed about our clothes; we tried to improve our appearance; we gossiped about each other; we read; we studied.

Religious Affiliations at the Sisters

Our instructions in matters of religion or catechism were administered exclusively in school, private or public. The parish lent a priest to take up this duty. Our Sisters merely required us to participate in mass twice weekly in their chapel, and on Sundays in St. Anna, the community church near us. We all had to go—no exceptions for religious preferences. We had to follow a dress code. No short sleeves, for example.

Religions other than Catholicism were never mentioned in our discussions at the Sisters or at school. I once overheard someone say that she bought clothes from the Jews on Saturdays somewhere in town. I did not know what she meant. My education in such matters, including anti-Semitism for example, took place years later in the United States in the form of books and articles I read, television programs I watched, and people I met and listened to.

Attic to the Cellar: Girls Becoming Women

Growing up was something we all did but in different stages. No one really helped us. We were not even much help to each other. We were too self-conscious. Wouldn't asking for help admit ignorance, failure to cope?

The Sisters never broached subjects that concerned our maturing, and we knew better than to ask them. So when one of us started menstruating, it was pretty much kept under wraps. Some of the girls piled their soiled panties on the bottom of their closet units to be dealt with when no one was around. I was a bit late in developing, so I looked with astonishment at the buckets filled with panties floating in pink-to-red water in the cellar, where the wash tubs were. Everyone simply washed the little laundry by hand and hung it up to dry in the wash area downstairs. When one of us wanted to purchase a sanitary napkin, the Sister reached beneath her apron to withdraw a little package from some deeply hidden compartment and handed it furtively to the recipient as if she were dealing with contraband merchandise.

When my time came, I did not always have the money to buy sanitary napkins. I used an old rag, pinning it with a safety pin inside my panties. The rag would not always stay put when I was walking or running. To my horror, it had a tendency to work loose and slip out. The only thing to do was not to acknowledge ownership and continue walking as if nothing had happened.

Snooping around in the attic once, clandestinely of course, I noticed various limp, snow-white garments pinned to clotheslines. I recognized the hoods, and the face and neck shields of the Sisters. These were the items they starched to perfection, rendering them as hard as cardboard, to be worn with their black habits. I also saw narrow, rectangular slips of cloth with ribbons attached at each end. I was sure they must have served as sanitary napkins, because the Sisters had no money of their own. They had to adhere to their vow of poverty. *How could they get those things so clean?* I wondered. I wish I could have asked them, because we had a difficult time cleaning our underwear.

Chapter V: Discipline

We learned to recognize the different Sisters by their walk, by the rhythm and click of their heels on the permanently polished floor, by the swish of their heavy skirts, by the rattle and clatter of their long string of wooden rosary beads. The speed of their steps indicated the seriousness of the situation. What was the offense? Has someone misspoken? Has someone raised her voice in an argument?

For various forms of misbehavior, work was sometimes used as punishment. These chores were normally performed by the nuns, but a culprit might find herself having to sweep the stairs in our three-story building, or operate one of the potato-peeling machines in the cellar.

But there were occasions when work was not used to discipline. When most of the girls had left for the weekend, those who stayed were often asked to take part in cleaning the parquet floor in the study halls.

That was the job I disliked the most. The herringbone-arranged panels formed long parallel lines in the halls. With a pad of steel wool beneath my foot, I scraped back and forth, one panel at a time, until it was judged clean. The chore seemed never-ending.

The nuns never laid hands on us in corporal punishment. They preferred making us feel guilty, with the intended psychological impact.

Verhör [Interrogation]

One serious case did cause consternation among us. A purse had been stolen. Certain girls were evidently considered suspects. I was one of them. Twelve of us had to line up, standing shoulder to shoulder in the large study hall. Sister Arilde closed the door behind us.

For quite some time, she stood facing us, wordless, locking her eyes into ours, then passing her gorgon-look from one girl to the other. She asked the first one in the row whether she was guilty.

"No" was the answer. And so it went down the line. Taking a few steps back, the Sister waited again. This time, she picked girls at random, repeating the question. The answers were still "No."

Then, she switched to yet another approach. Standing very close to me, she asked darkly: "What would your deceased foster mother say if she saw you here today?" I was struck dumb. The others were confronted with similar guilt-inducing tactics.

I had reached the point where I was almost ready to confess to a crime I had not committed, just to conclude this punishing session. Getting no result, the Sister finally gave up and dismissed us. We never heard whether the "thief" was found. The Sister told me later that, of all the girls, I looked the guiltiest. Perhaps my anger looked like guilt to her.

The experience left a permanent impression on me. I think of it today when I come across a war movie with prisoners subjected to interrogation.

Chapter VI: Becoming Ill

I can't say that I received gentle care from the nuns when I suffered a severe ear infection that prevented me once from attending a pre-Christmas event that was important to children at that time.

It was the St. Nikolaus fest that took place on December 6. According to custom, children needed to be cleansed of their misbehavior before Christmas. St. Nikolaus came to the house with his companion, Rumpus, a mean-looking, rag-covered individual carrying sticks and branches bound together, with which he beat the assembled children, while St. Nikolaus read aloud their misdeeds recorded in the golden book. So someone had indeed kept track of our sins during the year.

These were scary moments. Lying in bed with my sore ear, I heard the squealing and shouting in the hallways below. St. Nikolaus did not leave, however, without passing out some treats.

My ear infection must have been serious, because only in the most severe cases did the nuns allow us to skip school and remain in bed. A solid crust had completely sealed shut my left ear.

The day after St. Nikolaus, the abscess broke, and a stream of green and yellow pus flowed over my pillow. I was never given any kind of medication or pain relief. Calling a doctor was not even considered. A day later, I went back to school.

The Sisters judged the seriousness of a girl's illness by her appetite. "You can't be very ill as long as you are still eating," they used to say.

At the Clinic off Campus

Swollen tonsils used to plague me throughout my childhood, but one particular recurrence was deemed too severe to ignore. "Out they must come," the nuns decided.

Thirteen years old, with a very sore throat, I was dispatched to ride the tram by myself to the state-run outpatient clinic. There I encountered dark hallways crowded with sick people, some sitting on the floor, their backs propped against the bare, paint-peeling wall. I located the reception desk, where I had to answer some questions. Then I waited like the others.

When my turn came, a nurse took me by elevator to the operating room, a huge empty space with a high ceiling. In the middle squatted a large recliner. Above it, a blindingly bright light inside a hood hung suspended from the ceiling.

Sitting upright in that chair, I spied the doctor wrapped in white, wearing a head mirror as he was walking around the back of the room among tables with tools. On a roller table next to me, I anxiously eyed an assortment of shiny chrome medical instruments shaped like prongs, probes, and hooks.

With wide leather straps, the nurse secured my arms and

waist to the back of the chair. She tied my feet together and fastened my legs to the metal column of the movable base of the chair. I was trussed like a calf for slaughter. *Why all those precautions?* I wondered.

The nurse placed a white gown over me and a cap to cover my nose and lower face. A nearby dressing cabin had a plastic curtain with pictures of fish on it. She told me to let her know when the fish started "swimming." They did. I was out.

I awoke still strapped into that chair. One tonsil was gone. But there was still the other one to be removed. The doctor was bending over me holding an instrument resembling a silvery stick from which he drew out a retractable wire sling. He lowered the stick into my jacked-open mouth, caught the targeted tonsil number two, and pulled the sling tight to sever it. I had awakened too soon from anesthesia. Was the amount of ether still rationed in 1956?

My scream, more of a liquid gurgle, came out of my blood-filled throat. Despite the leather harness, I had managed to free one of my legs, which, in my fury, I punched into the good doctor's lap. I was vomiting blood over my lap and his. A string of expletives followed, from him. The nurse patted me dry and placed a thick cotton pad in my lap to soak up more spilled blood. She guided me to a recovery room, where all postoperative patients were crouched or seated on the floor. No chairs. When I was stable enough, I was sent to the tram station to return to the Sisters. I was looking forward to the ice cream I had been promised, but nothing had any flavor. In fact, I couldn't eat at all. For now, it was back to the bedroom.

In addition to tonsillitis, I used to be plagued by fever blisters and styes. Styes, in particular, caused a problem because the affected eye would swell almost shut. In his office, the doctor lanced the sores without anesthetic while I had to remain motionless.

Chapter VII: Christmas

We did believe in the magic of Christmas. And when the season brought the first snow, we greeted it with never-waning excitement, enchanted by waking up to a white landscape.

Christmas at the Sisters would not have been complete without our group's visit to the *Bayrische Nationalmuseum* [Bavarian National Museum] to view the exhibit of baroque-period nativity scenes, some dating to the eighteenth century. Today, it is still considered an extraordinary collection of finely modeled carvings of figurines dressed in period costumes of the Alpine region of origin, including crèche animals and elaborate background landscapes depicting native flora and fauna. The religious devotion shown in the life-like expressions crafted so long ago by human hands moved and inspired us. Among the crèches of varying sizes, we were especially intrigued by the miniatures that lacked no detail.

During the Advent season, the four weeks prior to Christmas, we made artful arrangements of fir branches fastened to small boards and decorated them with pine cones, artificial red berries, sparkling ribbons, and candles. These creations served as table centerpieces for the dining room tables and corner niches and nooks. One such artwork once caught fire after a burning candle had been left unattended in a small room. A Sister rushed in with a blanket and threw it over the entire table to extinguish the flames. The damage was limited to a black burn in the table center to remind us ever after to be careful with candles.

The season was a frantic time, with everyone working on a themed project for a gift, such as sewing or stitching a pillow cover for parents. Each year, someone came up with a new idea. Next season, it might be crocheting a small blanket.

The nuns, too, were busy behind the scenes. They sewed gifts for us by hand, maybe a cosmetic cape to be worn over the shoulders and tied around the neck. They wrapped each cape carefully, tied it with a silken ribbon, and presented one to each of us at the Christmas celebration.

It was a special moment indeed when it was time for us to enter the large study hall. We saw a beautiful floor-to-ceiling spruce commanding the center, simply but artfully decorated with hand-made straw ornaments and white candles that were burning. It smelled of warm tree resin, candle wax, and cinnamon cookies.

Chapter VIII: Attending School off Campus

I was the only one from the Sisters to attend a public grammar school, because the other girls attended a private Catholic school.

At this level, the public-school classroom was an equalizer of social differences up to a point, because academic standing outranked any such inequalities, such as appearance or pedigree. It even affected school friendships.

Our Teacher

I vividly remember these school years because of Betty Biederer, our only teacher, who taught all subjects. She stood about six feet tall in her angular frame, with long arms that vigorously gesticulated when explaining our lesson. Her deep voice boomed forth from a square, bony face framed by dark gray hair tied into a braid wound around her head.

Fräulein Biederer was a force. Everything she said mattered. We respected her. We feared her. We learned from her. She never let us forget that she was preparing us for our future. She brooked no foolishness. A classmate once allowed herself to read private material during class. When she evidently had come across a funny passage, she forgot where she was and laughed out loud in a short burst, cut short when Fräulein Biederer's steely look met the student's crimson face in rigor mortis.

The curriculum included cooking lessons. I looked forward to that class. As instructed, we prepared a prescribed meal with the labor strictly divided among us. In a special room designed as a kitchen, we chose from a variety of utensils. The surroundings were spotless until we delved into our specific tasks. On that occasion, we made spaghetti. I loved flattening the pasta dough and seeing thin sheets of it hanging like laundry on drying racks. I especially liked the camaraderie afterward while sharing the result of our labors. The bell rang. Class was over. Everyone quickly left for home, and I headed for the Sisters by myself.

Mittelschule [Middle School]

By 1956, I had completed the standard lower education grades (nine years) at the *Volksschule* [public school]. Following the advice of the Sisters, I took the next step. After passing a series of entrance examinations, I was now ready for an elective, gender-segregated public institution called Mittelschule für Mädchen am Salvatorplatz.

Mittelschule is not quite the same as junior high school in the United States, because the emphasis is on <u>elective</u>. Passing the Munich Education Department examinations in math, German language, history, and geography represented an important milestone in one's education.

Again, I was the only one from the Sisters to attend this school. It meant that I had no one to work with on the homework. It also meant that I felt like an outsider. My classmates knew each other from sharing similar family backgrounds and milieus. They formed their own groups of friends.

Our Teachers

Our math teacher, Fräulein Eberling, stood out for her beauty, impeccable grooming, and implacable facial expression. Her features were flawless, like a doll's. A single string of white pearls matched her elegantly understated apparel. She entered the classroom, tilted her mask-like face toward us without a hint of enthusiasm when explaining a lesson, and was impassive even when returning tests with disappointing results. Excitement only occurred in the hallway after an examination, when groups of us gathered comparing answers and methods of math problem-solving. My results often did not match the other students'. Their answers were correct. Mine were wrong.

Quite different in every way was Frau Reiterle, our physics teacher. Her dress was wrinkled, her slip always showed. She complemented her untidy appearance with an unpredictable demeanor. We could not fathom what exasperated her. Suddenly, her face became bloated while she spewed saliva-like foam through her buck teeth, shouting words of condemnation about our incompetence. A shudder went through the rows when she entered the classroom. Frau Reiterle discussed theory in a disconnected way, leaving us guessing. Was physics only abstract, or could it also be concrete?

Our geography teacher, Fräulein Hoffmann, was very progressive, encouraging us to pay a visit to the nearby university to familiarize ourselves with that institution. Making such a private visit never occurred to us. We felt we did not belong there, at least not yet. She was unrelenting in her demands on us. We had to draw meticulous maps and even locate remote towns in foreign countries. Fräulein Hoffmann was such an imperious presence that when she called me to the dais to present my well-researched report on Japan, I froze. I simply could not speak. She told me to go back to my seat. I received a D grade.

Business subjects, including typing and shorthand, were Frau Hamlin's specialty. She was kind to us. I learned easily and performed well on tests, even though I did not have access to a typewriter for practice at the Sisters. The excellent training I received in these business subjects allowed me to support myself later.

Frau Riegler, the head of the administration, was a squarely built middle-aged lady, about as wide as she was tall. She was *energisch* [determined]. She was definitely in charge. We seldom saw her. But Vati, my foster father, made her acquaintance. Vati was still living by himself in Tivoli then, but he made a special effort to speak with Frau Riegler. Our class was scheduled to participate in a school outing requiring a fee, which neither the Sisters nor my foster father could afford. Instead of taking part in the outing, I had to attend a class from another teacher, according to administrative rules. Vati thought that I should be allowed to stay home with the Sisters instead. He was incensed. He considered the school's answer a form of discrimination. Frau Riegler stood firm. Their conversation became heated. Vati could not contain himself and ended up leveling at her some of his most repulsive profanities. She won. I had to join another class. I noticed that thereafter the teachers treated me with a certain coolness.

Our only male teacher in *Mittelschule* was a corpulent monk of the Franciscan order, who belonged to the parish of St. Anna. He was responsible for our religious instruction. One of the students, Anne, clearly affected him. She was a pretty girl and physically extraordinarily mature for her age. She did not seem to be aware of it, but he was. Whenever she asked a question, his chubby face turned beet-red. He began to sweat and became flustered. Try as he might, he couldn't help himself. The rest of us noticed but just snickered. That's as far as it went. But a few months later, a different instructor came to our class. Had the diocese removed the monk, or had he asked for a transfer to save himself?

In 1959, my school days in Munich came to an end. The academic competition among students during that three-year program at *Mittelschule* was fierce. I felt intimidated by the teachers and by the students. My diploma shows an overall B minus grade.

Chapter IX: Music in My Life

Singing practice was my favorite activity at the Sisters. The occasional overtones in our *a capella* choir transported me to a momentary sirenic realm. We must have looked almost angelic standing together in harmony, a modern version of the singers depicted in the 1420s Ghent Altarpiece.

I wanted more music, so I joined the local choir in the St. Anna Kirche. We practiced mostly simple hymns. On Sundays, I looked forward to listening to solo organ music that preceded and ended the mass. I especially liked the end, when the full-throttle pipes accompanied us through the open portal and down the stone steps, sending us home. Little did I know that I was listening to Bach preludes.

Munich had many churches with choirs. The one belonging to St. Michael's on the Neuhauser Strasse was famous for its challenging music program offered every Sunday. It was often recorded and broadcast over the radio. I decided to audition at a choral practice.

The choir director, Herr Lautner, was a corpulent middle-aged gentleman of pleasant demeanor, short of stature, always dressed in an ill-fitting suit, white dress shirt, and tie. The audition consisted of my repeating the notes he played on the piano in the practice room, while the chorus members listened, followed by my singing a song of choice. Then he handed me a piece of sheet music to sing that contained a selection unknown to me. I did not know how to read music, so I faked my way through the measures by gauging the up-and-down of the notes' notation, as I had done at the Sisters. I managed to pass and was allowed to join the other singers when their practice began.

My amateur music education began in earnest at St. Michael's church with its ambitious program. We sang masses composed by Mozart, Haydn, and Schubert with a full orchestra, or we sang small selections of hymns by Bach and Handel, accompanied by an organist. The music reached its pinnacle at festivals such as Easter and Christmas, when an additional trumpet choir would blast forth from opposite sides of the balconies above, the sounds ricocheting from the ornately decorated baroque ceiling and walls, enough to bring me close to fainting. Schubert was my favorite composer, because one could sing him. His music offered surprises in subtle ways. By moving just a single note in a chord, he changed the melody from lilting to heartbreaking.

When mass ended, Herr Lautner, drenched in sweat, heaved off the podium, his suit jacket showing large dark areas below his armpits. Was I ever invited to sing a solo at St. Michael's church? That was the prerogative of the choir director's girlfriend. He coached her well. Several choir members had voices superior to hers, but that's not how it worked. However, just to be exposed to that level of music and to be part of it made for the happiest moments in my life at that time.

Concert tickets I could not afford. Instead, on my way home from *Mittelschule*, I lingered in front of the music store on the Maximilianstrasse. Among a couple of plaster heads of well-known musicians, the shop window displayed the title pages of instrumental compositions and operas by famous composers. I memorized the titles of works and names of composers and performers.

Many years later, at a university music library in the United States, I appreciated the privilege of being able to listen to a record or tape playing a concerto, with the music score at my side.

I have always taken my singing ability for granted. Singing was easy. I learned how difficult it was to learn to play an instrument when I started taking my first piano lessons in my late forties. The frustration I experienced learning to read notes, while trying to coordinate left-hand and right-hand keyboard finger movements, overwhelmed me.

What would my violinist father say about my practicing this late in life "First Lessons in Bach," a book meant for children?

My fingers barely spread to an octave. I have not reached the stage where I can <u>hear</u> the notes just by looking at the sheet music, or <u>see</u> the notes while I am playing without the sheet music, but at least I have progressed enough to be able to sing along while I am playing a simple piece.

Music, like nature, was my joy and inspiration. Music transported me to another realm. That in itself made it relevant. I did not try to reason with music nor with nature. I could not explain them, but they made me happy. They let me forget sad and lonely moments.

Chapter X: Working Girl

Two years before I graduated from *Mittelschule*, one of the Sisters recommended to me an off-campus typing assignment. It was for a well-connected young lady who would pay well. I was flattered.

I was fourteen years old and had just finished my first year of typing instruction. I was a slow but conscientious typist. With no typewriter of my own, I could practice only during class. The Sister was aware of the degree of my capabilities, so I accepted the offer without asking for further job descriptions.

With the provided address in hand, I set off for the tram station. I had to transfer a couple of times and then walk to find my way in that unfamiliar part of town.

It was Christmastime. Snow-covered branches of huge fir trees lining the streets hung low and heavy. Thick snow blanketed the twelve-foot-tall hedges hiding the houses beyond, and snow from the cleared sidewalks was piled high against the stone walls surrounding the villas.

My footsteps and tiny, fan-shaped, feathery scratches of bird feet were the only markings on the pathways. No one else was in sight. Light snow was falling. Silence. I had been transported to an enchanting neighborhood.

The house in question was a three-story villa behind an elaborate iron gate with its spikes wearing snowcaps. A shiny brass plaque fastened to one of the gate's stone pillars spelled "Dip.-Ing. Dr. Herbert Meyer" in black letters. Lining the driveway to the house were large, uneven white lumps of spirea, with only a few spindly branches protruding here and there from the snow.

The villa exhibited all of the characteristics befitting that exclusive district: Massive stucco walls, iron-barred windows on the ground floor, a huge wooden entry door connected to a speaker system and buzzer operated from within, tall mullioned windows on the upper floors, a slanted mansard roof, and a curved stone terrace on the side of the house leading to the parterre, suggesting what must have been formal flower beds in temperate seasons, all against a background of well-placed large shade trees, now dark and leafless.

The setting was beautiful in a heavy, somber way. It could have been from a contemporary version of a Grimms fairy tale. I felt like I was in a time warp.

I rang. The intercom buzzed. I identified myself. The door opened. In those surroundings, I expected to see a maid wearing the customary black-and-white uniform that they still wore at that time. Instead, I saw a lady wearing a common cotton housedress held by a large kitchen apron. She looked to be in her early sixties but could have been younger. She was tall, bent over slightly, haggard actually. She crossed one of her arms over her chest, the other reaching to the side of her face trying to remove stray gray hair loosened from the knot in her nape. Her thin face expressed discomfort, if not fear. She asked me to enter.

"First, we'll have lunch," she said almost inaudibly, and motioned me to follow her into the dining room.

As we passed the wide vestibule and the adjoining rooms, the few pieces of mahogany furniture standing about seemed dwarfed in that space. The ceiling was high, the walls empty, the windows bare. I felt cold.

A young woman came toward us. "My daughter, Monika," the lady said by way of an introduction, her face brightening suddenly. The mother, then, was Frau Meyer.

Monika was a bright-looking young lady in her early twenties, who studied at the university. So that's the one for whom I was to type.

Striding purposefully toward us now was a corpulent gentleman in his late fifties, sparse hair glued to his white scalp, his serious mien shadowed by bushy eyebrows and beady black eyes. A two-inch scar sliced above his right cheekbone toward his eyes, a status-symbol reminder of his student fencing days, signified that he had not flinched from his opponent's assault. He was wedged in a shiny black suit with slacks marked by a sharp, perfect crease. His black polished shoes showed mere remnants of worn-down heels. A white long-sleeved shirt from which French cuffs without cufflinks protruded from the jacket. No tie. The collar and the cuffs of his shirt were gleaming white but frayed. No money for a new shirt or cufflinks or shoe repair? Frau Meyer could only see to his sartorial needs, such as washing, starching, and ironing his shirts?

This, then, was the Dipl.-Ing. Dr. Herbert Meyer. Where did he work? What exactly did he do? Where was his office? His comportment befitted his title, his vestments not quite.

With averted eyes, he offered a curt *Guten Tag* and passed us on his way to the dining room. We followed. He sat down first at the head of the expansive table. Monika and I took our seats on opposite sides. I felt lost, just the three of us, hands in our laps, shadows of our faces reflected in the high polish of the tabletop. The fourth place setting at the other end was reserved for Frau Meyer. She served lunch.

The servings were delicious but certainly not opulent. No one asked for a second helping. Would there have been any available? The lunch consisted of vegetable soup followed by a green salad. The main dish contained pieces of stewed meat with potatoes and carrots. Frau Meyer filled our glasses with water from the tap.

Lunch was a silent affair. We concentrated on the plates in front of us. Like everyone else, I was trying not to make a sound, not with my table setting, not with chewing or swallowing. The atmosphere was stifling.

Frau Meyer did all the work herself, unobtrusively, from bringing the food to clearing the dishes afterward. I saw no sign of hired help; her calloused hands testified to that. Nor did the daughter assist her. Mother may have been the chatelaine, but she was also the maid.

Who were these people I was facing? Were they still shadowed by that terrible war? What had Dipl.-Ing. Dr. Meyer done during the war? How did they manage to be in this villa? Has it always been theirs? Or had the family just moved here? Were they refugees? If so, where had they come from? Were the pieces of furniture salvaged from a previous abode? Though there was no sign of war damage in that part of town—not even shrapnel tracings—the damage was incised in the parents' faces, in their demeanor, in the strained formality of person and place, in the emptiness.

With one exception: Monika. From the minute I met her, I saw her facial expression and movements full of life. Her grooming exhibited care and expensive taste. She was young. Did Monika's overt presence stand in for the parents' repression of war-time experiences? Was the daughter her parents' investment in the future?

After lunch, Monika led me upstairs to her quarters. What a different sight, compared to the rest of the house. Her apartment occupied the entire area below the roof. The angles of the mansard construction allowed for unusual spaces. The colorful and bright arrangement of a sofa and chairs with pillows contrasted with the bare downstairs area I had passed through. Her room presented a spring-like picture that differed from the wintery scene outside her windows.

Now the typing task was awaiting me at her desk. The job at hand, her seminar assignment I was told, involved typing an essay of about twenty-five pages on colored paper, with spaces left for her artwork, a rather creative approach. Sheets of different-colored paper were stacked on one side of the manual Adler-brand typewriter, her handwritten pages on the other.

Monika leaned over my left shoulder, her beautiful

chestnut locks brushing against my side as she watched me type. When I had trouble making out her scrawled instructions, she interpreted. The typed lines were to be of irregular length, both horizontally and vertically, to accommodate a drawing here, a collage there. I was to follow strict instructions, matching text with paper of a specific color. This assignment would have been a challenge for even the most experienced typist. I summoned my courage and continued.

I typed slowly, carefully, moving my eyes back and forth between the handwritten sheet on the left and the one in front of me in the typewriter. Typing on white paper without making errors was hard enough, but on colored paper? Any erasure would eliminate the color and leave a white spot on the sheet. And what was I supposed to use for an eraser? Monika looked all over to find one, without luck. Did she herself know how to type? Did she even need to know?

My head started to spin, my fingers became sweaty and unsteady. I realized that I had committed myself to a task for which I was ill prepared, but I was too scared to speak up, too intimidated by Monika's glamour. I started over again a number of times, but it was obvious that the job was simply too big for me. After several failed attempts, even the positively inclined Monika decided to stop.

As I got ready to leave, I was actually paid. I don't recall the amount. I did not deserve it and said so. In the end, I did accept the money—rather sheepishly.

I walked away defeated from the typing assignment. I felt alienated in that group of people, in that villa, in that neighborhood. I was out of my league in every way.

But above all, I was conflicted. I had passed from storybook surroundings into a house hiding mismatched occupants and interior, a house where the present collided with the past. I could not answer my own questions or resolve my doubts. I could not match the pieces in the puzzle.

The question about the typing job, however, was resolved some weeks later. The Sister, my referring agent, mentioned that Monika had her essay typed by her father's secretary. Through the grapevine, I heard that this job offer had first been extended to another girl, a more experienced typist, who—savvier than I was—had the good sense to pass on the proposition.

My Next Typing Jobs

In 1959, as a sixteen-year-old graduate of *Mittelschule*, I was still at the Sisters when I began full-time work as a stenographer in a patent attorney's office.

I had an exacting boss with the title Dipl.-Ing. Dr. Braun, a certified engineer. He was a gentleman beyond his sixties with wavy gray hair always in need of cutting. Continually chewing the flat, spittle-wet end of a cigar, he gave orders in a mild voice that hid his steely attention to the work at hand. Glancing at me from several feet away, he could tell that, among three sheets of carbon paper, I had inserted one page incorrectly into my typewriter. We still used carbon copy paper, then, which required skill in making neat corrections on multiple sheets of paper.

The most respected person in the office was the head

secretary, Andrea, whose job consisted of typing patent agreements and contracts. She had to type *fehlerfrei* [letter perfectly]. According to legal rules, then, she was not allowed to make a single erasure. If she did make an error, she had to retype that page all over again. Andrea demonstrated utmost concentration. The rest of us had to behave appropriately. No chatting. Our salaries were paid in cash every month.

The best part of my duties was going to the Munich patent office to research and verify patent listings in tiny print in huge bound books stacked tightly on tall shelves that were often beyond my reach.

For me, it meant getting away from the chained-to-the-typing-desk routine and trading it for the rapid page-turning, book-cover-slapping atmosphere in the patent building, as every clerk or attorney sifted quickly through the library material for his office.

A year later, in 1960, I left the patent office to work in a large insurance company.

It turned out to be more than a job change, though. It was a new working environment with a looser work ethic and more casual camaraderie. The administrators worked in bullpens and considered the typists fair game, albeit more in a humorous way. During the lunch hour, colleagues passed around photos showing them standing next to a Volkswagen—or better—rented for a weekend, creating a faux semblance of ownership.

These pictures were destined for out-of-town relatives or friends as proof of improved economic status. In transportation—be it walking and using the tram, or owning a bicycle, a Vespa, or even a car—each step, however small, made a difference.

There was a lightheartedness now at work. But at the end of the day, I still had to return to the Sisters. Although things were changing there, too.

Chapter XI: Toward the End

Life began to change, even for those of us confined to the Heim. I noticed that several girls had boyfriends. One was already a young lady. She studied ballet. Wearing her blond hair tied into a taut ballerina bun, she tiptoed down the hallway in diaphanous pastel wraps floating like veils behind her.

Several young men, with cars, vied for her attention, which she seemed to take for granted. A car was an ace; few owned one.

I wondered how such relationships came about. Some of the girls met young men through their brothers. How did the others do it? It was a mystery to me.

A more important change meant leaving the Sisters. Our age group was getting ready to fly the coop. By then, most came away with firm opinions about their experience at the nuns.

Some of the girls swore they would never return for a visit. They had disliked the discipline and the regimentation. Others wished to be married some day in the Sisters' private chapel they knew so well, possibly owing to the religious atmosphere.

Many of the girls I had known were already gone. They had left so hurriedly that I was left without future contacts. I do not know what has become of them, with the exception of my friend, Gertaud. We, too, would lose track of each other for a time in the years to come.

But after I had emigrated to the United States, and after her mother's efforts to find me, we began our lifelong correspondence.

For the majority of the residents, the stay at the St. Anna Heim was merely temporary, for a year, more or less. I spent seven years there, more than anyone else I knew. Those years had been formative for me.

First, by accepting me, the Sisters had helped me overcome my difficult childhood beginnings in Tivoli. My foster parents had kept me for many years despite their precarious circumstances, saving me from a worse fate in a city orphanage and from a shaky future. They had shared their bread with me. They couldn't have done more. The St. Anna Heim provided a stable environment under the caring eyes of the nuns.

Second, I owe my future development to the Sisters. They had encouraged me to continue my education in *Mittelschule*, because it gave me a means to support myself at the age of sixteen.

Third, the St. Anna Heim gave me friends, girls of my age with whom I could form friendships, with whom I could share thoughts, with whom I could laugh.

From that day forward, I was responsible for my own room and board. I could no longer rely on the Sisters, nor on my foster father. I was expected to hold my own. Would I be able to make wise decisions?

The St. Anna Heim still stands today. It is a nursery school now, a day-care center, called Haus für Kinder.

PART III: MY BIRTH MOTHER - A PORTRAIT

My most difficult task is writing about my birth mother. I can't recall any substantive interchange between us because her occasional presence in my life did not encourage a bond. It was precisely her absence that left wounds. How could I talk about us? There was no narrative, no family history she shared with me.

After my birth mother's death, I was astounded to learn, by chance, that I had relatives in the United States. After contacting my newly found cousins, they passed on to me the fragmentary family history.

My mother's ancestors were German and French. I heard that her German grandfather, August, served in the Franco-Prussian War (1870-71). Wounded, he recuperated in a French field hospital, where he met Marie Luise, a French nurse, whom he married. The family moved to Landsberg am Lech, a town in Swabia, Germany.

In Landsberg, August owned and operated a *Gärtnerei* [nursery] located on the main road leading out of town. In the vicinity was a large house on an acreage owned by Ludwig II of Bavaria (1845-86), the "mad king." August was commissioned periodically to take care of portions of those grounds to plant seasonal flowers and such. Someone in the extended family is said to have a photo showing King Ludwig II with his small entourage which included the gardener, August, and Marie Luise.

When I visited my birth mother in 2003, I noticed on her kitchenette wall a picture of August, my great-grandfather. It showed him wearing a jaunty Loden hat (Loden is boiled wool), a jacket, and Lederhosen. A mustache twirled up at the ends crowned his merry lips. He was steering a raft down a river somewhere in Bavaria, a recreational activity that many still pursue today. When I pointed to the picture, my mother's only disjointed words referred to his facility for languages. I wish I could have known him.

When I was a nascent teenager visiting my mother over an occasional weekend in the 1950s, she spoke to me only once about her other children.

I learned that I had an older half-sister from a different father. My mother had tried to abort her, she stated brutally, by jumping off various pieces of furniture. But *"Wenn's der Herrgott will, must Du's ham* [If the Good Lord wills it, you'll have to have it]," she sighed. She gave her to foster parents; she did not elaborate. End of discussion.

I was number two. Did she try to abort me, too, and when that failed, she eagerly handed me over to strangers? She must have been successful with number three, because she said, "*A Bub wär's g'wesn* [It would have been a boy]." So I would have had, should have had, a brother from the same father. I think about that sometimes. What would he have been like? What would it be like to have a brother?

Once or twice, my mother came breezing into my foster parents' humble Tivoli hut in the 1950s. Like a fairy she was, the flounce of her expensive skirt swishing away any dust on our sofa, her high heels clicking nervously on our bare, rough wooden floorboards, the fresh scent of American "Ponds" cream wafting about her person. She seemed to be a creature like those depicted in beauty posters pasted on advertising columns on sidewalks or in magazines lined up in newsstands. She was pretty, high-spirited, and charismatic when in the company of adults. But I was a child. I could not connect with her, nor she with me. I had the distinct feeling that she did not know what to do with me.

My mother was hard-working with an each-dog-for-himself attitude, keeping her money to herself. It could have been no secret to her how we lived. Did she ever reimburse my foster parents for my care? Not to my knowledge. Yet, my foster parents never failed to acknowledge her as my mother and insisted that I do the same.

She did, however, send me an annual Christmas package. My birthday is around that time, too, which made it handy to celebrate two occasions as one. The package was sent for general delivery to the Tivoli mill gatehouse near us. How many trips did I make to check whether it had arrived? It usually came at the last minute, but it did come.

One time, it contained a very special gift. It was a beautiful bisque doll with real blond hair and two perfect white teeth protruding between its red lips. With pliers, I pulled out her two front teeth, playing dentist. Was I willfully destructive or angry that I was not as pretty nor as well dressed as that doll? Was I born ornery, or was I just becoming so? Vati, annoyed by my behavior, took the doll away from me, hid it, and gave me instead a piece of cut wood to play with. I never saw that doll again.

One time, my birth mother took all of us to a café in Munich. Off in a corner in the lobby, comic books were arranged on a display spindle. I noticed a "Donald Duck" booklet in German. My mother bought it for me. I read it threadbare. It did not depict Donald Duck but showed instead an obscenely rich Dagobert Duck (Scrooge McDuck or Uncle Scrooge), who had spied a flyspeck on the windshield of his black limousine. Instead of having his car washed, he decided to trade it for a new one. That brought him even more profit because he owned the factory that made the cars. Reading that booklet allowed me to escape into a world of fantasy.

Sometime in the 1950s, with my birth father still declared missing from the war, my mother married a carpenter from the Bavarian village of Farchant, near Garmisch-Partenkirchen. Together they built a house there.

When I told an elementary school acquaintance that my mother was building a house, she called me a liar. "There is no way that could be true," she said.

It was inconceivable to her that my mother was rich enough to build a house during those times, while I was considered one of the poorest girls in class.

When I was about fourteen years old, I visited my mother

on rare occasions in Farchant just for a day or two during school vacations. I did not feel comfortable being with a mother I did not know well, nor being with a stepfather I did not know at all.

For years in the 1950s and 1960s, she used her house for a *Zimmer-frei* (bed-and-breakfast establishment) for tourists. When I stayed with her, my job was to help with chores. In the early morning, I bicycled to the village bakery to purchase fresh rolls, butter, and jam for her guests.

Once, I rode my mother's bike to the store while I was having my period. Unbeknownst to me, I was bleeding heavily through my underwear.

When I parked the bike by the store, a farmer's wife stopped me, pointing out the huge red spot covering the entire rear of my dress. She helped wrap the skirt part of my Dirndl dress around me as best as she could to hide the splotch so that I could ride home without further incident.

I felt uneasy around my new stepfather. Instead of dropping my used comfort pad in the bin below the kitchen sink where everyone might see it, I wrapped it tightly in newspaper and hid it in my purse to dispose of during my next outing to the village. Without my knowledge, my mother decided to go through my purse and found the little package. *Why did she do that? What did she expect to find?* She was appalled at what she found, slapped me, and called me *schmutzig* [dirty].

When my foster mother died in 1952, my birth mother did not attend the funeral, nor did she send any condolences. Neither was she involved in placing me in the St. Anna Heim with the Catholic Sisters in Munich, where I spent the next seven years.

By the time I arrived in the United States in 1961, I had completely lost contact with my birth mother. I felt no tie to her. I was not doing well in my new country. I could only find jobs as a house cleaner until my English improved, qualifying me finally for office work. I did not wish to explain my new circumstances to her.

Over the years, I searched in the library for her name in her town's phone directory. As long as she was listed with her husband, and as long as she had her house with the same old address, I assumed she was alright.

I thought about writing to her but could not summon the courage. That only became harder with passing years. Forty years later, and after her husband had died unbeknownst to me, I was able to re-establish contact with her. She had never tried to find me.

Would my mother have been a different person had it not been for the war? Did that war leave anyone untouched?

My Mother as Legal Guardian
During my youth, my mother remained my legal guardian, because my foster parents never formally adopted me. That meant she would have had to sign legal documents on my behalf. The need never arose. But there was one occasion toward the end of my stay in Munich in 1959-1960 that did require her signature: A document relating to my forthcoming emigration to the United States to join my fiancé, whom I had met shortly after leaving the Sisters.

My fiancé took care of my visa requirements. All I needed

now was a passport. That meant that my mother had to sign the requisite application form. I had to come up with a plan to do that.

Traveling through western European countries did not require a passport at that time, except to Eastern-Bloc countries such as Yugoslavia. It was not unusual, then, for Germans to vacation on the Adriatic in cities like Split. I could get away with pretending to my mother that I needed a passport to spend a few days in Yugoslavia.

Why not explain to her the real reason for going? I could envision the skirmish that such a revelation would have caused. It would have been futile. When it came to questions of parental supervision, my mother became imperious playing her role—the outcome unpredictable. I did not trust her.

But I had to see her in person to get what I wanted. With the application form in hand, I took the train from Munich to the village of Farchant and then walked to her house. The typically short conversations between us extended that time to a question-and-answer session about my reason for wanting to go to Yugoslavia. I lied. I got my passport.

What did I gain from my devil's bargain? An emigration I had not sought, a marriage I had not sought, a life I had not sought.

PART IV: EMIGRATION TO THE UNITED STATES

I didn't want to go. I couldn't speak the language. I didn't really know the man, nor did he know me. We had known each other only for a few weeks. He brought the ring. All of a sudden, I was engaged. How did this happen?

It was a beautiful fall, an Indian summer. I was eighteen years old and had just moved from the Catholic Sisters to a private room I rented from a widow in an apartment house paid for with earnings from my secretarial job in the insurance office. Perhaps now I could arrange for private singing lessons on Saturdays. I was still daydreaming, hoping to pursue my music education.

A chance meeting with Tom, a young American, led to developments I was ill-prepared to handle. A first encounter. I felt flattered. It quickly became serious.

Then, all courage left me. I wanted out. I wanted him to go away. Besides, he had told me of his friend, Richard, who was always reading, carrying a book around wherever he went. *What was he reading?* I wondered. I wanted to meet him, but I did not have the courage to tell Tom that I was more interested in his friend than in him. Communicating only with a bilingual dictionary and sign language did not make things easier. I felt trapped. I felt weak. So I just followed along meekly.

One day, Tom, who had quickly become my fiancé, brought me the forms for an Americana visa application. *That should solve the problem for me bureaucratically,* I thought, because I could never furnish the required information, such as my Hungarian father's whereabouts (still declared missing). Surely, I would never qualify for a visa.

Part of the application process was an interview scheduled at the American Consulate located near the Haus der Kunst museum. Mine was conducted by a carefully groomed middle-aged American lady with eyeglasses dangling from a glitzy strap.

She called me into her office, asking in German sundry questions based on papers she was holding in her hand. One of the questions related to illegal activity such as prostitution.

Did I grasp what she was asking me? In shock and confusion, I must have mumbled a satisfactory answer. She smiled, a bit embarrassed, as if to apologize for having to ask such an egregious question.

A few months later, the visa arrived in the mail. It was beautiful, with a formal stamp and a red ribbon, or was it blue? Tom had also borrowed the money through his mother in California to pay for my overseas flight to the United States.

"I don't want to go," I pleaded again with Vati, my foster father, who was still in Tivoli.

"Du musst auslöffeln, was Du Dir eingebrockt hast [You must finish what you started]," he said firmly.

New York-Reno-Red Bluff

On an early morning in March 1961, I said goodbye to Vati in Tivoli, with one large, awkward suitcase containing all my earthly belongings, a purse, and a bunch of spring flowers, which were a going-away gift from my former officemates in the insurance company where I had worked last.

One more time, I looked back over my shoulder at the frost-covered meadow, mist hanging in the tree branches, our hut half-hidden by bare fruit trees and stalky bushes, the sun coming up halfway just as Vati had carved it in his war-time wood panels depicting fleeing families from the east.

I comforted myself thinking, *Come spring, the trees over there in the United States must still be green like ours. It can't be all that different.* Nothing prepared me, though, for the coming culture shock upending my life at age eighteen.

I flew alone, my first airplane ride, on a discounted ticket for immigrants on KLM from Munich over Amsterdam to New York. We flew over snowed-in Newfoundland, where I watched from the fish-eye window a single car wending its way along a road. No other visible life. It looked lonely.

But there was life in New York at Idlewild Airport, as it was called then. Inside, it was warm. There were escalators and huge silently moving automatic glass doors. A customs official took the orange I had been holding during the flight. No fruit could be brought into California—my ultimate destination—I learned later. My first disappointment: He took it from me without giving something back.

Would my fiancé be there to meet me? What if he didn't show up? My total net worth was $100.00 hidden in my purse. How far would that get me in New York City, without a single friend or relative?

But he was there. He had left Munich ahead of me and was waiting for me. He took me by the hand, and we hustled to the Greyhound bus depot in the city to leave with the next bus headed to Reno, Nevada. What a new experience it was to ride across this new territory, squeezed together on the back seat for several days and nights.

Once in Reno, he led me straight to the courthouse for a marriage license, he explained. But where to get married? There were plenty of wedding chapels around for that purpose, which we could not afford. Perhaps through the help of the lady at the courthouse, Tom located a preacher, his wife, and another gentleman willing to serve as witnesses. We got married immediately.

The "ceremony" took place, I assume, in the preacher's house. Before we started, Tom spelled out, through sign language, the procedure to follow. At the appropriate moment, namely when he poked me with his elbow, I was to say, "Yes." Once more, I did as I was told. I was in over my head.

I knew next to nothing about my husband and even less about his family—only that he had one in California. How much can be discussed without language?

Tom had notified his mother in Red Bluff, asking her to pick us up in Reno the same evening in a borrowed car. In a battered, bilious-green 1956 Ford, his entire family arrived: His mother, two grown brothers, and two little sisters. What was awaiting me next?

We drove through the night to my mother-in-law's house. That was the honeymoon trip. It was not without its charms. The car's headlights lit up the weeds bordering the highway: Tall green grasses, like the ones depicted on Easter-egg-coloring booklets displayed in drugstores in Munich in that season. Green grass in early March? Of course, I was in California now.

Her house in Redding was a small bungalow cluttered with window screens I had never seen. The doors were left unlocked all night. Chicken wire fence surrounded the weedy yard. A lone orange tree grew in a corner. Cars lined the street in front of the house. We left our belongings in ours, unlocked.

"No one will bother it," my mother-in-law confirmed, surprised at my question.

The days now unwound with little coordination or planning. Life seemed easy-going in a sweet kind of way, even if it was a bit slovenly.

I admired my mother-in-law's culinary arts. Her fried chicken was the best I had ever tasted. Dirty dishes stayed in the sink for a while unless I washed them right away. I made a diligent, yet ineffective, attempt at bringing some order into the household.

My new abode was, to some degree, better than the one I had left behind in Tivoli. Both looked poor, but with the difference that the hut in Munich was ramshackle due to privation, while the one in California was due to benign neglect.

My new in-law family patiently suffered my attempts at speaking English. I spent much time observing and listening to relatives, neighbors, and shoppers in the stores. My vocabulary increased. Venting my frustration to my mother-in-law about her casually run household, I even had the audacity to drop a snide remark in my newly acquired English once or twice, which she took with equanimity in her Arkansas twang.

I was a culture shock to them, as they were to me.

Home Sickness, Loneliness

I missed familiar surroundings, sights, sounds, and smells. The housing styles were different, and so were the yards and the way they were kept, as were different neighborhood shops with sundry kinds of merchandise unfamiliar to me. Even the streets were not the same—no sidewalks in some cases. The cars didn't sound the same, nor did their horns. Even the emergency vehicles did not have the familiar tritone I remembered from Munich.

And I missed the flora. I saw palm trees now, but I did not see any chestnut or linden trees in their spring beauty.

The seasons were a bit askew. Autumn oak leaves dropped in spring with new buds already forming; last season's oranges still hung on the tree branches with budding May blossoms adjacent to them; roses, iris, tulips all bloomed at once and in the same spring season. In the summer, I became homesick whenever I saw a larkspur or cosmos in the corner of a yard.

I missed watching a summer rain, a thunderstorm in August.

I missed hearing the deep sonorous sound of the church bells that used to ring at certain hours in my hometown.

I missed seeing the Romanesque, baroque exteriors, and rococo interiors of Munich's churches.

I missed listening to the Bach preludes played by the organist at the beginning and end of Catholic masses, not to mention the performance of Haydn and Mozart masses on Sundays and church holidays.

I missed certain foods and the smell of fresh leavened bread. As Bertolt Brecht, the German playwright, was supposed to have complained during his hiatus in Santa Monica in the 1940s, "One can't even get a decent loaf of bread here."[18] He objected to the soft white, sliced loaves sealed in plastic. I tried to bake German cakes, which resulted in utter failure because I did not realize that the flour here is different from that in Europe.

I missed my foster family, or what was left of them.

I missed the companionship I had shared for seven years at the Sisters at the St. Anna Heim.

I missed looking forward to special occasions, be they Easter, Christmas, the first of May (*der 1. Mai*). In Munich on those days, we tried to have a special meal by whatever means. We put on better clothes of whatever type. We commemorated the holiday in some way by visiting the

---

[18] Mary Ann Niemczura, Dr., "German Bread," "You can't get proper bread in the States," WordPress.com, February 19, 2016.

botanical garden or the zoo or simply by conversing at length about past pleasant times. We took a break from the everyday. But now, all days seemed more or less alike. And the stores were always open.

I lost the thread between past and present.

I missed order in my life. It was so untidy now.

I lacked plans for the future.

It was *Stunde Null* [zero hour]. Where do I go from here?

Desperation

Tom decided that the two of us should move to Tacoma, Washington, to start a new life. Once there, a pleasant landlady rented us a small room with a hotplate consisting of two burners for cooking.

But I soon realized that my husband was very ill psychologically. He could not keep a job. He required hospitalization. His family on welfare could not help. We did not know anyone in Tacoma. We were barely acquainted with our apartment house neighbors. All of a sudden, I had become the mainstay of our two-person family. I was in a new country, in a new town, without family support, without English language skills.

I was stunned. I couldn't go back to Tivoli, and I couldn't return to the Sisters. They all had done their part to help me grow up. Nor would I have had the money for a return plane ticket. I was on my own.

What would my future be? How would I work through each day? I couldn't even share my troubles with anyone. Who was there to listen to me, say a kind word, offer advice?

While my husband wrestled with his psychological illness, I wrestled with depression. I destroyed photos, letters, and whatever few physical reminders I had saved from my past. I felt empty, hollowed out.

Working

In searching for answers, I considered some kind of employment. A job would enforce a schedule that would make me get out of my box, go to work, show up on time, be reasonably groomed, and be alert to perform my duties. For part of the day at least, it would force me to concentrate on something other than my personal problems. I would interact with other people. I was convinced that more than one life has been saved by a job.

Hoping that I would find work with just my typing skills, I walked into the unemployment office, as it was called then. How cordial everyone was in that office. Instead of being confronted with the expected snarly bureaucrat, I sat across from a polite lady who advised me that typing skills alone would not suffice. "You need more than that—shorthand, for example," she said, with a benign smile.

But even typing presented hurdles, as I found out quickly in a pre-employment test. The German and American keyboards are not quite the same. Due to linguistic differences—English lacks the German umlauts, for example—the American keyboard has a couple of differently placed letter keys. It is an exasperating experience for a fast typist, as I was, to make that adjustment overnight.

While I worked on improving my skills on a borrowed

typewriter, I applied for a waitress opening at a nearby café. I didn't let my lack of English stop me. I thought patrons could always point to the food offering listed on the menu, and I would go from there. The hardest part was to bellow out the order in top voice to the cook behind the counter: "Two eggs over easy, two bacon, and one ham on the side." I just couldn't do it. I asked one of the other waitresses to do that for me. At the end of the day, I was fired. I was paid nothing, even though I had helped deliver and serve lunch to about twenty members of a women's club earlier that day, carrying many heavy trays with beautifully prepared sandwiches from the restaurant.

Job number two materialized soon thereafter. I was part of a group of women hired to operate pressing machines in a dry cleaners. That meant two women per machine: One operated the push button for the hot, heavy metal lid, while the other laid out the garment beneath it. It was steamy, dangerous work, because once activated, the lid dropped quickly—better not to have hands in the way. At the end of that day, each worker was paid $1.00. Then we were fired. Our job had been to clear out all accumulated dry-cleaning orders before the boss closed the business for good.

Job number three lasted almost a year. The unemployment office referred me to my first typing job, a one-man insurance company. The owner was a cantankerous older man, short and stocky, with a gravelly voice, bulging eyes in a fat, round face that made him look like a toad. A trusted secretary had been with him for years, while a string of office clerks had come and gone due to his sudden voluble outbursts.

I was the newest hire assigned to follow instructions on bookkeeping and typing business letters. "For heaven sakes, don't let her (referring to me with a nod) answer the phone," he hollered to my compatriots. My English had improved by then, but I still had trouble understanding what someone was telling me over the phone.

Remembering the advice about shorthand that I had received at the unemployment office, I wanted to learn the English version based on the German system I had learned at the *Mittelschule* in Munich. I decided to write to Gertraud, my girlfriend from the Catholic Sisters, asking her to send me the requisite booklet.

With those instructions at hand, I was now able to teach myself English shorthand by listening to and writing down radio broadcasts in our apartment. A year later, in my first steno job at a bank, I often carried home my steno pad to decipher the dictation notes I had taken earlier in the office. In those evenings, I was often in tears, because I had trouble transliterating my shorthand. I was trying to learn a new shorthand system while still trying to learn English.

Learning English

I missed my mother tongue. I could not state my intentions precisely, nor did I know how to ask for advice. I could not express myself, exchange thoughts and ideas as I wished. Beyond my reach was language as a link to other kinds of knowledge. But even at the basic level, communication requires an equal partner. Who would want to talk to me anyway?

How, then, did I learn English? I basically "picked it up" by listening. There was no ESL (English as a Second Language) assistance available as there is today. I was still ignorant of the American public library system. How could I ask for something I didn't know existed?

But there was television. We had a used one in our one-room apartment. When it stopped working, my husband showed me what to do. The innards of a TV at that time contained glass tubes inserted into a circuit board. A nearby drugstore had an apparatus on which I could test the removable tubes of our TV to see which one needed to be replaced. Once repaired with new tubes from the drugstore, I was able to watch programs such as *Queen for a Day,* and *What's My Line?* I recall the pretty lady, "Kitty," one of the moderators in *What's My Line?* She wore an elegant black dress with white transparent sleeves that looked like wings, or large seashells. I could not follow the dialog and thought the shows were rather strange. But I kept watching and learning.

Very slowly, I found my bearings through my improved English skills, allowing me to communicate better and adjust to my new surroundings. I was beginning to understand American culture. I learned that "How do you do?" is not an invitation to expound on my well-being and that "You must come and see me sometime" is not an invitation to an impromptu visit, regardless of the friendly tone of the speaker.

And once I discovered the American public library system, I was on my way. Following the example of Frank McCourt, the late Irish American author, who became a steady patron of the New York City Public Library, I became a grateful and steady borrower at my local city library branch.[19]

My husband was not well, and my English skills were still at a minimum. Reading became not only my learning aid but also my panacea for loneliness and depression. To this day, when I become deeply involved in a story, and I have to interrupt my reading to look up a word in a dictionary, I have trouble finding my reading passage again. It is as if while reading, the letters had walked off the page and had become real people, things, and phenomena. Now getting back to my reading passage, the letters must return once more to their ordered, sober existence of black symbols on a white page. Momentarily, my life had become part of an imaginary stage set.

A year or so later, I signed up for night classes at a junior college. Because of work, I was able to enroll in only one course at a time. Somehow, I had passed the grammar test, allowing me to enroll in English Composition 101. For our assignments, we read and wrote about Albert Camus, his thoughts on nihilism and the absurd. Did I really belong in that class? Daunted by my lack of education, I tried to make up for lost time. I read library material until I fell asleep in my chair. But I kept going. I am still learning.

---

[19] "Frank McCourt speaks on education teaching," The Tufts Daily, April 29, 2004.

Conclusion: My Ambivalence about Germany

I will never be able to escape the ever-present shadow of the German war legacy. Yet, I feel ambivalent because of the unspeakable horror experienced by the victims on both sides, on all sides.

My ambivalence is due to my awareness that I owe my existence to foster parents who had been avid Hitler supporters. Although they were just barely surviving themselves, they took me in as an orphan. They did not forsake me, as my birth mother had done.

And there are the associations between present and past that my mind forms instantly. Today, I feel a momentary gut-wrench every time I see on television a team of United States basketball players enter an arena in a trot. It is their trot that disturbs me, because that is the same jog with which a group of German men once emerged from their cells, entering a cellar in Berlin to be hanged. They had been accused of participating in the attempt on Hitler's life on July 20, 1944.

An old TV broadcast I saw sometime in the 1960s shows them dressed only in warm-up pants, lining up against a wall before being hanged by piano wires strung up on meat hooks. They were formerly ardent Hitler supporters who had turned traitors to him. To others, they became heroes and martyrs.[20]

Among the martyrs are also individuals, like Georg Elser[21], the National Socialist Resister, who used his horologist's skill to fashion, single-handedly, a bomb meant to destroy a speaking platform for Hitler in Munich in 1939.

The Germans have tried to bury their past and have moved on. For the older generation, *Vergangenheitsbewältigung* [managing the past] is still a work-in-progress, as exemplified by the slowness in bringing to justice people implicated in war crimes. The former war participants are now in their late nineties. Those still alive will no longer be held accountable due to their age.

Dealing with the past on another level is Robert Probst's[22] review of Anna Corsten's dissertation, *"Unbequeme Erinnerer,"* [uncomfortable reminders] (now available in hardcover). He describes how after 1945 members of the West German *Historiker Zunft* [Guild of Historians] fought against acknowledging the Holocaust findings of their United States colleagues.

No different was the initial reluctant response of museums, or any government supported agency, to the

---

[20] "Trials of the men and women involved in the attempt on Adolf Hitler's life in July, 1944," Library of Congress.

[21] Cord Aschenbrenner. Rezension, Das Politische Buch, "Der Attentäter von der Ostalb," Süddeutsche Zeitung, 11. Juni 2023.

[22] Robert Probst, Rezension, Das Politische Buch, "Der präzise Blick der Außenseiter." "Holocaust-Forschung nach 1945. Präziser Blick der Außenseiter," Süddeutsche Zeitung, 25. Juni 2023.

recovery of stolen art during the Nazi era. The Gurlitt[23] collection found in 2013 in a Munich apartment was such a case. But great strides have been made since in that direction.[24]

And although German schools continue to actively engage the young in the process of *Aufklärung* [enlightenment] by taking groups to visit Auschwitz, for example, the present generation is no longer willing to carry the burden of the old. After all, the younger ones did not take part in past crimes and brutalities.

But this raises the question: Are we able to be selective about our emotional legacy? Galit Atlas, the American psychoanalyst and author, declared in an interview with Vera Schroeder that we cannot deny that we are the children of our parents and grandparents in all of our psychological heritage.[25] My case may serve as an example; mine is a cumulative description and analysis of handed down experiences from my foster parents and my own remembrances.

In dealing with my personal *Vergangenheitsbewältigung*, I remind myself, or am reminded, of the war's legacy, as in the case of *Stolpersteine* [pavers].[26] In some German cities today,

[23] Sophie Gilbert, "The Persistent Crime of Nazi-Looted Art," The Atlantic, March 11, 2018.

[24] Kirsten Grieshaber, "On a mission to return heirlooms Nazis stole," Los Angeles Times, July 5, 2023.

[25] Vera Schroeder Interview, "Jede Familie trägt die Geschichte eines Traumas in sich," Süddeutsche Zeitung, May 26, 2023.

[26] Nicole Glass, Editor, "Stolpersteine: Stumbling Into History," The Week in Germany (German Mission in the United States), January 17, 2018.

pavers with vital statistics engraved in them are inserted in sidewalks near the last residences of the Jewish victims prior to their arrest and deportation.

Not only Jews are commemorated in the *Stolpersteine*. In 1992, the German artist Gunter Demnig inserted the first such incised stones in Köln. He wanted to memorialize the Sinti and Roma victims during the Nazi era. Today, the stones include all groups who were persecuted—homosexuals, euthanasia victims, political and religious martyrs, such as Jehovah's Witnesses. Even survivors of concentration camps are listed, as well as those who fled to the United States, Israel, and other countries. Demnig's individual stones are a reaction to the anonymization of mass murder. Even so, Katja Petrowskaja, the Russian author, remarked in a symposium at a Book Festival in Berkeley, California, in May 2019, that deep individual suffering may cause us to overlook the big picture of historic significance.[27]

Unaccounted for in our memory are individuals and groups, Germans and foreigners, who are not memorialized in history books or in public spheres despite Germany's many efforts to pay tribute to them today. Are there just too many to remember?

Who knows the names and number of prisoners of war of various nationalities, Russian soldiers, for instance, who were massacred under German supervision?

Who knows the names and number of forced laborers who

[27] Katja Petrowskaja, Bay Area Book Festival in Berkeley, California. "Wunderbar Together," Pavilion of German-American Friendship, May 4, 2019.

were abducted from their homes and from their countries to serve in the German war effort, to serve in German households, like those who worked for my foster parents in Salzgitter? And those who were exploited by German firms, like the Reimann[28] case discussed in the *The New York Times* in March 2019, or the Bahlsen food company in Hannover described by Veronika Wulf?[29] Bahlsen's twenty-six-year-old granddaughter, Verena, was overheard whitewashing the treatment of forced laborers in her grandparents' factory during the war. The next day, social media created what the Germans call a *Shitstorm*. Under pressure, Verena from Bahlsen offered *"missglückte Entschuldigung* [apologies for having misspoken]." An outside group is now investigating the company's employment history. What do other family members have to say about their company's war history? Social media is making it more difficult to hide today.

It is noteworthy, though, that while a part of today's generation is not willing to share the psychological freight of the past, some young people are beginning to show a true interest in the lives of their elders.[30]

The Past Intrudes on the Present: Germany Today

One such reminder of the war is the discovery of *Blindgänger* [undetonated bombs], not to mention tons of

---

[28] Katrin Bennhold, "Germany's Second-Richest Family Discovers a Dark Nazi Past," The New York Times, March 25, 2019.

[29] Veronika Wulf, "Kekshersteller lässt seine Geschichte seiner Zwangsarbeiter aufarbeiten," Süddeutsche Zeitung, May 16, 2019.

[30] C. J. Schüler, "Unpacking my Grandparents' Books," October 17, 2022.

ammunition, still hiding underground in some West German cities. According to an online report[31] specialists defuse about a thousand such bombs a year. Each time, hundreds of residents have to be evacuated at great inconvenience and expense.

On a more personal level, some war survivors have developed immunity to adversity to such a degree that they react to present-day life-threatening situations in unexpected ways. Reported recently in a town in northwest Germany, an eighty-two-year-old shopkeeper was robbed in her store and held at gunpoint by two young masked men. "Stop this nonsense," she said, "I don't scare easily—not after what I experienced during the war."

Attitudes and reactions to past events differ between generations (old vs. young) and between locations (West vs. East Germany). For the older generation, those over sixty, there is the historical—perhaps historic—amnesia, of both war damage inflicted and damage endured.

On damage inflicted, some movie theaters in Germany showed a documentary, *Der unbekannte Soldat* [The Unknown Soldier][32] of the active involvement of the *Wehrmacht* [common soldiers] in war atrocities. The reaction was swift and unprecedented. "Those crimes were committed by the Nazis, not by the Wehrmacht," viewers insisted repeatedly in local reporter interviews. They refused to believe what they

[31] Feargus O'Sullivan, "World War II Bombs Still Pose a Threat to German Cities," Bloomberg, June 3, 2019.
[32] Michael Verhoeven, Producer and Director of Dokumentarfilm, "Der Unbekannte Soldat," Deutschland 2005/2006.

saw. Their anger was so vitriolic that the footage was quickly removed from the theaters.

On damage endured, having lived for two generations under a Communist regime, the East Germans look upon the Hitler regime as some evil manufactured by the West. Accordingly, they saw themselves as victims, such as in the bombing of Dresden in 1945, not as perpetrators.

During my visit to Munich in 1964, I overheard shreds of a conversation in a café, which must have been arguments between two generations about the war. The daughter confronted her parents with the often-heard question: "How could you have stood by while…" with the elders responding, "Only those who lived through those times know what it was really like."

Controversies arise today about new issues that separate generations ideologically. The influx of refugees into Germany from parts of the Near East, the Maghreb region and other areas, and now Ukraine, is of concern. At first, West Germans, particularly the young, welcomed refugees with food, clothing, blankets, and toys for the children. They were truly sympathetic to the newcomers and showed a genuine interest in those who had fled their countries, while many East Germans began to fear trouble, citing potential incidents of crime.

The express commitment to do "good" at all levels can range from helping refugees to helping small animals. In the city of Bensheim, one such case described how a young rat stuck in a manhole cover was extricated by a crew of eight professional animal rescuers and volunteer firemen. "Even such animals that are hated deserve respect," one rescuer said. Not all Bensheimers agreed.[33]

Conflicting elements of past and present beliefs are clouding the political future. The Far-Right movement has gained considerable support. Its success is astounding and frightening.[34] And there are still some who probably would do today what they did during the war if they had a chance.

The past casts its shadow even over art. Recently, a foundation revealed the Nazi sympathies of the late German expressionist painter Emil Nolde (1867-1956). Angela Merkel, the former German Chancellor, decided to remove his paintings from her office. Bernhard Fulda, a Cambridge historian who examined the foundation's archive, remarked, "The German past is a complex one. There is guilt, there is complicity, there is looking away, there is beauty."[35] B. Fulda is speaking for me.

What It Means to Be German

What constitutes German-ness? What makes one German genetically, geographically, historically? I have to qualify my German-ness as follows: German mother, Hungarian father, French-German ancestors on my mother's side, Hungarians on my father's side. I was born and brought up in Munich.

How do People Classify Me?

---

[33] "Kleine Ratte, große Aktion: Ratte aus Gullydeckel befreit," Süddeutsche Zeitung, Februar 25, 2019, Direkt aus dem dpa-Newskanal.

[34] Erika Solomon, "As German Worries About Future Rise, Far-Right Party Surges," The New York Times, June 21, 2023.

[35] Peter H. Koepf, "Why Angela Merkel has banned two paintings from the chancellery," Arts & Life, April 2019.

In the United States, I am considered German. In Germany, I am considered American. In both cases, I am surrounded by the negative aura associated with each country, with Germany's negative war reputation in the United States, and with America's self-importance and domineering stance in Germany. Do we have anything to say about when, where, and to whom we are born?

Instead of saying I am German, I proffer my Bavarian birthright. After all, I am a *Münchner Kindl* [a native child of Munich], that is, having been born in Munich, I am one of its own and not a *Zuagroaste* [someone who has migrated from somewhere else].

Today, Bavaria conjures up positive images of a smiling President Obama[36] drinking beer with the locals in the village of Krün in 2015. It conjures up pleasant thoughts of the annual Oktoberfest in Munich, which now requires a reservation to enter one of those overcrowded *Bierzelts* [beer halls]. The fest is a major tourist attraction on an international scale.

In my youth, I used to hate the place: The overflowing beer mugs, the bellowing and bawling of the revelers, the ear-worm melodies played on the festival rides. The only things I liked were the instantly melt-on-your-tongue cotton candy, and, if I was lucky, some green grapes.

More to my liking are the iconic symbols of Bavaria. They elicit thoughts of wandering alongside alpine meadows with

---

[36] "Obama, Merkel celebrate U.S.-Germany friendship at G7 summit," PBS News Weekend, June 7, 2015.

local wildflowers, such as the singularly blue Enzian, the red Alpenrose, or, much higher up among the rocks, the Edelweiß which is hard to find, and even harder to collect, because it grows only on the most craggy outcrops. The story goes that more than one young man has lost his balance, if not his life, climbing high up in the granite, trying to capture a rare Edelweiß for his beloved.

Meadows evoke images of mountain paths with periodic *Wallfahrt* [pilgrim] rest stops. At the edge of a path, a traveler usually finds a carved wooden crucifix about eight feet tall. Nailed together at the top, forming a V-shaped "roof," are two wooden slats leading down, one on each side, ending at the middle of the cross. Attached at Jesus Christ's feet is the customary container for flowers meant to be filled with wild flora that a wanderer may have picked from the surrounding meadows. It's a good spot to stand and meditate for a while or pray.

But the Bavarian image is after all only a part of Germany and German-ness. There is, of course, the national characteristic of maintaining order and keeping records. My birth certificate may serve as an example. It shows more than just my birth date. Next to it are two more lines with blank entries: *Heirat* [marriage], and *Tod* [death].

Because I got married in the United States, the line for *Heirat* is still bank. And so is the one for *Tod*. As I plan to live in my adopted country till death, the last one, too, will stay blank.

If I had remained in Germany, my life would be summarized in just these bare three dates on a card in one of those fat, sturdy Leitz-brand file folders on some German bureaucrat's desk.

"*Ordnung muß sein* [Order is necessary]," so the saying goes, which means, of course, that one has to follow orders. I thought I did.

While visiting an outstanding exhibit of African art in the *Stiftung Preussischer Kulturbesitz* [Prussian Cultural Heritage Foundation] in one of Berlin's museums in 1989, I suddenly heard someone approach me in a fast clip from behind. It was the museum guard.

He asked me point blank to remove my hands from my winter coat pockets.

"*Das ist nicht erlaubt hier* [That is not allowed here]," he said in a tone that made me forget to swallow.

I thought, *Why doesn't he just shoot me?*

My startled reaction made me realize that I am more American now than German, that my sharp German corners have been slowly chiseled off after having lived more than sixty years in the United States.

In his life and work, W. G. Sebald, the late German novelist and essayist, wrestled with what it means to be German. After spending many years in England, and after returning to Germany for repeated, periodic stays, his ambivalence only increased.[37] I share that ambivalence despite my periodic longings for my birthplace.

Ambivalence aside, one must take the long view and

---

[37] Catherine Edwards, "We look at the preoccupations that drove the literary works of German emigrant writer W.G.," Culture Trip, December 26, 2016.

consider more than just recent changes, namely all the developments over the last century or so that have made Germany the nation of global standing that it is today.[38]

---

[38] Rethinking German history: "A world elsewhere"/"Germany in the World," by David Blackbourn, reviewed in The Economist, July 1, 2023.

Epilogue: A Poem Dedicated to All Refugees

Composed and translated by the author.

"Vatis Schnitzereien"

Aus Holz geschnitzt mit einem Klappmesser
Groß wie ein Buch, wie eine Bibel
Hält er das dunkelgelbe Holzstück aufrecht
Wiegt es auf seinen Knien
Schaut es lange an
Und spricht
"So war es."

Mit seinem Messer zieht er die Spur der Landstraße nach
Auf der sich die Flüchtlinge langsam zu bewegen scheinen
Jung, alt, Männer, Frauen, Kinder, ein paar Babys
Vorgebeugt, gebückt, stehen geblieben, rückwärts schauend
In die Heimat
Immer vorwärts

Handkarren schiebend, Ochsenwagen antreibend,

Elisabeth Haggblade

Hochgestapelt mit Kisten, Eimer, Körbe,
Stühle, Tische, Schränke,
Betten, Kissen, Wäsche,
Mäntel, Kleider
Mit Seil umspannt
Hier und da
Kreuz und quer
In Eile

Morgen früh war es
Die Sonne ging schon auf
Links unten im Bild strahlt sie schon
Über den Waldrand, die Felder
Zu beiden Seiten des Landwegs
Dicht stehen die Weizenähren im Feld
Dicht folgen die Flüchtlinge aufeinander
Auf der Landstraße bis zum Horizont
Oben rechts am Ende der Holztafel

So spricht Vati zu mir
Dem kleinen Mädchen
An sein Knie anlehnend
Gebeugt über sein Handwerk
Die große Holztafel
Mit der lebendig gewordenen Menschheit
Die Völkerwanderung des Jahrhunderts.

"Vati's Wood Carvings"

Carved from wood with a pocketknife
Tall like a book, like the Bible
He is holding upright the dark yellow wood piece
Cradles it on his knees
Contemplates it for a long time
And says
"That's how it was."

With his knife he draws the path of the country road
On which the refugees seem to move slowly
Young, old, men, women, children, a few babies
Leaning forward, bent, standing still, looking backward
To the homeland
Always forward

Pushing hand carts, motioning forward ox carts
Piled high with crates, buckets, baskets,
Chairs, tables, wardrobes
Beds, pillows, linens,
Coats, dresses
Tied with rope
Here and there
Every which way
In haste

Early morning it was,
The sun already rose

Shining in the lower left in the picture
Above the forest edge, the fields
On both sides of the country road
Thick stands the wheat in the field
Tight follow the refugees each other
On the country road reaching toward the horizon
In the upper right of the wood panel

So speaks Vati to me
The little girl
Leaning against his knee
Bent over his handiwork
The big wooden panel
With the humanity that has become alive
The migration of the century.

Acknowledgments

I would like to express my appreciation to:

Mr. Vince Font, Owner and Chief Editor of Glass Spider Publishing;

The late Dr. Helen Gordon for reviewing and editing parts of my first draft;

And above all, the late Dr. Berle Haggblade, my husband, for encouraging me to write and for accompanying me on this journey.

About the Author

Born in 1942 in Munich, Germany, Elisabeth Haggblade immigrated to the United States in 1961. She received her PhD in English Philology from the Free University Berlin. Retired from teaching part-time English and Linguistics, the author currently lives in Santa Barbara, California.

Visit her website at www.trauteroseauthor.com.